the

GOOD

the

BAD

and the

BEAUTIFUL

a handbook to marriage

G. WRIGHT DOYLE

Torchflame Books
An imprint of Light Messages

Durham, NC

Copyright © 2018 George Wright Doyle

The Good, the Bad, and the Beautiful: A Handbook to Marriage
George Wright Doyle
www.reachingchineseworldwide.org
wright.doyle@gmail.com

Published 2018, by Torchflame Books
   an Imprint of Light Messages
www.lightmessages.com
Durham, NC 27713 USA
SAN: 920-9298

Paperback ISBN: 978-1-61153-293-7
E-book ISBN: 978-1-61153-292-0
Library of Congress Control Number: 2018944725

All Scripture quotations are taken from the *New King James
Version* of the Bible. Broadman & Holman Publishers, Nashville,
Tennessee, 1996

PRAISE FOR THE GOOD THE BAD AND THE BEAUTIFUL

"This simple yet elegant book invites contemporary readers into a rich conversation with a patient and compassionate mentor. G. Wright Doyle wrote it with the most pressing and realistic needs of Christian couples in mind. Apart from biblical principles, he enacts the daily dramas and challenges in the marriage scene with a reflective insider's view. Like a *Pilgrim's Progress* for married couples, no matter how long you have been married, Doyle's book condenses a journey with profound biblical wisdom on the good, the bad and the beautiful, as men and women in marriage are called to experience the deepest mystery and beauty of God's plan for creation."
—Li Ma, PhD., Research Fellow of the Henry Institute for the Study of Christianity and Politics, Calvin College, Author of *Surviving the State, Remaking the Church*

"Doyle deals with the specifics that need attention for all our marriages, but all of them are placed before the wisdom, the intention, and the commitment of God for husbands and wives. Doyle's wife, Dori, has signed off on this book with her approval, a major tribute in itself. She is a woman of faith and joy in the Lord, and a devoted partner happy to be married to the man who has written this book on marriage. How wonderful to have a book that reflects their sound marriage and directs us to God's lessons for each of us."
—Rev. Tad de Bordenave, Anglican Church or Nigeria, Author of *The Year of Paul's Reversal* (Best Man at the Doyles' wedding)

"A treasure chest of Biblical truth, personal and pastoral experience and stirring encouragement! God's Word is clear. Doyle's application is clear and concise. But those seeking successful and fulfilling marriage, or the restoration of a failing one, will find meaning and hope in the joys of learning and practicing God's blessed plan to become more and more like His Son and their Lord."
—The Rev. Peter R. Doyle, ThD, DD, Author of *Jonathan Edwards on the New Birth in the Spirit*

CONTENTS

INTRODUCTION

For some time, I thought of writing down a few observations about marriage, but held back. My hesitation sprang from a variety of sources. So many books about marriage already fill the stores; do we need another? And they are mostly written by experts—people who have spent years doing scientific research about what makes couples happy or sad, how to build a better relationship, how to avoid infidelity and divorce. The books I list at the end have been especially helpful to me.

As I have re-read them, I have wondered, "Do I really need to write a book on marriage?" I am not an expert. Then there is my own marriage, marred in past years by multiple maladjustments, and still far from ideal. I can't set myself up as the perfect example to follow, so why should I presume to share any of my ideas with others?

To add to my doubts, I reflect on the fact that few men read books about marriage, and yet much of the happiness of any marital relationship stems from the attitudes and actions of the husband. If the man leads, the woman will often (though not always) follow. A loving husband will prevent most problems from arising and will effectively—even if imperfectly—deal with the inevitable difficulties that come when two sinners live together.

Nevertheless, I am convinced that I should at least try to pass on some of what I have learned over the past fifty-one years since my wife Dori and I became engaged. Before marriage, we were required by my brother Peter, who performed our wedding ceremony, to read *A Handbook to Marriage*, by Theodore Bovet. Funny how I thought that, having read that one book, I had all the knowledge necessary for a successful marriage! But some of his words have come back to me since then, casting a beam of light upon an otherwise confusing path.

About two dozen other volumes on marriage have also proven helpful to me along the way. For example, Willard Harley's *His Needs, Her Needs* comes to mind, though I don't agree with all that he says.[1] One theme that keeps recurring in that book is the huge disconnect between dating (or courtship) and marriage itself. Repeatedly, Harley shows how people change radically after they say their wedding vows, and how terribly shocked and disappointed most couples are when the "honeymoon" period comes to a crashing close and the harsh reality of daily life together sets in.

I guess that is one of my main motivations for writing this handbook. I want to help others to think through what happens when two people tie the matrimonial knot, so that they won't imagine that something strange has happened to them when they encounter the usual trials of living together as man and wife. If possible, of course, I would hope that I could alleviate, or even prevent, unnecessary pain. I say "unnecessary," because so much of the sorrow that usually attends marriage can be avoided, both by wise choices before the wedding (or even before engagement) and by quick action when obstacles arise in our path.

More recently, Timothy Keller, with his wife Kathy, has given us perhaps the best all-around Christian treatment of marriage, *The Meaning of Marriage*. In fact, after reading it, I doubted whether I should publish mine! He has done a great deal of research, much of which disproves many common assumptions.

For example, "All surveys tell us that the number of married people who say they are 'very happy' in their marriages is high – about 61-62 percent." And of marriages that were not happy,

---

1   For example, he says that you can "divorce-proof" your marriage. Though his advice will certainly make divorce less likely, nothing but God's protection can prevent divorce. His title, too, speaks of "needs," whereas we don't really "need" anything but God and his love. And he claims that sex is "the one thing he can't do without," but many husbands have had to "do without" sex for shorter or longer periods of time, and have been able to survive and even flourish in their marriages. Still, I find much of what he writes quote useful.

"two-thirds ... will become happy within five years if people stay married and do not get divorced ... . [P]eople who are married consistently show much higher degrees of satisfaction with their lives than those who are single, divorced, or living with a partner."[2]

Then I realized that I discuss some things that others, not even Keller, don't, and that God seems to have given me something unique to say.

Our own experience has included going through almost a dozen years of marital counseling during the first thirty years of our marriage. As a minister, missionary, and friend, I have counseled others, often with Dori's help. These experiences, plus the books I have read, form the backdrop of much of what I now believe about marriage, but I hope that the Scriptures will provide the basic outline, structure, and even content of the main ideas that follow.

There won't be many stories to illustrate these principles, just the basic information. The works I recommend later are filled with anecdotes and examples, so I don't feel a great need to lengthen this little handbook unnecessarily. We will be looking at God's original plan for marriage— "the Good"—then at some of the causes of conflict, confusion, and collapse—"the Bad"—and finally, at what God can do with those married people who love, trust, and follow him—"the Beautiful."

At the outset, I should say that specific advice about handling finances, keeping house, sexual relations, bringing up children, and other very important matters will not be found here. My focus will be on the relationship between husband and wife, for from this will flow the motivation, energy, and wisdom to deal with all the problems and challenges that married couples face. Unless we make this relationship our main concern, all our efforts in other areas of married life will be out of balance and ultimately unsuccessful.

With those disclaimers, then, I offer this brief introduction to marriage with the prayer that God will use it to bring real happiness to couples of all ages and in all stages.

---

2   Keller, *The Meaning of Marriage*, 19.

Acknowledgements

No book comes from the mind of the author alone, not least a treatise on marriage. I am indebted not only to the authors whose works I recommend, but to countless Christian couples who have modeled faithful Christian marriage for Dori and me.

More particularly, I gladly acknowledge my debt to a few people who have, humanly speaking, supplied the guidance, wisdom, prayers, and encouragement that have enabled us to remain on this narrow but immensely fulfilling journey together.

Not to omit others, but to give special recognition to them, I thank:

My brother Peter Reese Doyle, M.Div., Th.D., D.D., who with his wife Sally Ann has not only set for us the "gold standard" of a Christian marriage, but who introduced us to Christian marriage, performed our wedding ceremony, and has counseled me over five decades. Peter read the entire manuscript and offered suggestions for improvement.

The late Reverend Lee Copeland, M.Div., M.A., a faithful pastor, wise counselor and marvelous Christian friend until his unexpectedly early death.

The Rev. John F. Kuebler, M. DIV., MA., who counseled Dori and me for three years right after we returned from Taiwan in 1989, helping us to recover from some serious relational wounds and setting us on the path to a healthier relationship.

The Rev. Tom Parsons, M.Div., Dori's brother-in-law, who gave her advice at a critical time in our courtship and who has been a loving friend and godly mentor to me for the past fifty years; and his wife, Dori's sister Jean, who has provided essential support and constant prayer for a wife married to a very difficult man. Tom has also read the manuscript.

Our daughter Sarah, who has shown us in her own life a pattern of a godly wife.

My wife Dori, who has stayed with me all these years, prayed for me, loved both me and our daughter, and consistently nurtured an intimate relationship with Christ. She also carefully read the manuscript and offered extremely useful comments, on the basis of which I made many revisions to the text, even omitting an entire chapter.

DEDICATION

Authors regularly thank their wives for their patience during the long process of writing. For reasons that will become obvious throughout this book, my debt to Dori throughout more than fifty happy years together is incalculable. As her name (Dorothy: "Gift from God") indicates, she is, aside from God himself, by far the greatest blessing bestowed on me in this life.

To my beloved Dori,
I've said it before, and I'll say it again.
As far as I am concerned,
"Many daughters have done excellently,
but you excel them all."
Proverbs 31:29

CHAPTER ONE

THE GOOD:
GOD'S ORIGINAL PLAN FOR
MARRIAGE

We must begin with the question, why does marriage matter? After all, a huge number of men and women live together without getting married, and countless others decide to split up after being married for a while. Clearly, both groups believe that something else is more important than the marriage bond.

Indeed, multitudes of married people behave as if they think that marriage is less important than fulfillment and success at work, making money, pleasure and entertainment, popularity, power, or relationships with other people, especially parents and children. After investing huge amounts of time, money and energy in courtship, they turn their attention to other, apparently more pressing concerns. The husband-wife relationship takes a back seat, though perhaps lip service may be given to its putative priority.

Often the forces that push marriage off the pinnacle of significance reside deep within the heart, where hopes and fears, disappointment and anger, pride and passion, laziness and selfishness drown out the voice of love. In our heads, we know that we should put our marriage first, but our hearts boil with conflicting emotions that prevent us from fulfilling our wedding vows. So, why is marriage important? Why is this relationship so special, and deserving of far more concentrated thought and effort than we usually devote to it?

In God's Image

The answer to this question starts with the very opening passage of the Bible, where the Hebrew words have profound implications for how we should view the male-female relationship. "In the beginning God created the heavens and the earth."[3] Although it may at first seem overly technical, it is vital to note that the subject of this sentence, "God," is *Elohim* in Hebrew, a noun that is in the plural here. But, contrary to normal grammatical usage, the verb "created" is singular in form. Something strange is going on; what is it?

Further light upon this anomaly comes later in the same chapter, where God says, "'Let Us make man in Our image, according to Our likeness; let them have dominion ... over all the earth and over every creeping thing that creeps on the earth.' So God created man in his *own* image; in the image of God he created him; male and female he created them."[4]

In this well-known passage, God (*Elohim* again) has one image or likeness, and the verbs, "said" and "created" are singular, but he refers to himself in the plural with the pronouns "Us" and "Our." Some Bible commentators say that God is using the plural of majesty, like a king who says, "We are not amused." Others claim that he is talking to the angels, but the passage then tells us that the image of God, though one "man," is also somehow more than one: "male and female," "them." So, both God and his image are singular and plural at the same time.

Many Christians have long believed that we have here an intimation of what later became the doctrine of the Trinity. After all, early in Genesis we read of God, and his Spirit, and his speaking.[5] Are these hints of Father, Spirit, and the creating Word that became flesh?[6] I believe so.

---

3   Gen 1:1.
4   Gen 1:26-27. In the *New King James Version*, words in English that are added to the original Hebrew or Greek for clarity are placed in italics.
5   Gen 1:2, 3.
6   John 1:3.

At any rate, Moses teaches in this very first chapter of the Bible that the union of man and wife somehow reflects the very nature of God. Man and woman together is (or are) the image of God. Theologians have debated what this means. Karl Barth is famous for postulating that the male/female relationship is the essence of God's image. Others believe that the image of God in man involves intelligence, communication, will, love, moral capacity, and more. Either way, however, we must conclude that the combined unity and plurality of man and woman somehow corresponds to the very being of God himself, and that their communion—involving all the elements that are usually included in the concept of "image of God"—somehow flow from the nature of God himself, in whose likeness both they and their relationship are created.

This puts a vast premium upon the man-woman relationship, especially the form it takes in marriage. Here we find one "unit," which we call a "couple." If they maintain this unity in a spirit of love, then they are walking, breathing representations of God, who the Bible says is love itself (or better yet, himself).[7] So, marriage possesses priceless value, for it somehow represents in fleshly form the invisible character of God.

Mutual Admiration

Perhaps this kind of unity explains the immense attraction men and women have to each other. After all, we cannot deny the fascination, even obsession, that lovers hold for their beloved. Love songs, poems, and the adoring couple across from you at the table in the restaurant, lost in wonder and oblivious to all around them—all testify to the all-powerful force of *eros*[8] in the throes of romantic love.

Delight: Love begins with delight. We delight in another's appearance, gestures, tone of voice, facial expressions. We like their ideas, their humor, their way of speaking. We enjoy them as

---

7   1 John 4:8.
8   *Eros*: Sexual drive, romantic passion, infatuation, from Eros, the Greek god of love.

people. We also respect them for their accomplishments, abilities, and especially their values and virtues.

Some cynics attribute all of this to hormonal activity, but physical causes only account for physical effects, so this explanation only tells us a bit about the emotions lovers feel, not their mental state. Should we say, then, with the psychologists and psychiatrists that romantic love represents the longing for a lost (or never enjoyed) intimacy with one's parent of the opposite sex? Or are we driven mostly by some fantasy, an image of the perfect mate, to which our current companion approximates just enough to evoke all the wonder and thrill of finding the one who will make us happy?

Yes, perhaps. But there is more, I think. It seems to me that the starry-eyed couple gazing into one another's eyes, totally absorbed in the beauty of the person across the table, are responding, at least in part, to something very real and true to our deepest nature. If we are all created in the image of God, and if the two sexes somehow mirror the beauty and glory of God in a unique fashion, then our appreciation, even adoration, of persons of the other sex derives from their resemblance, at least in part, to God himself.

After all, the Greeks and Romans depicted their gods as extraordinarily beautiful human beings, and we praise their lovely statues to this day. Maybe they were on to something, despite their silly idolatry. Though Christians do not believe that God has a body (the Bible says that he is Spirit),[9] something in the bodily form, and much more in the moral character, mental richness, and expressions of love of which we are capable, makes us walking representations of our Maker. I believe that our mutual admiration, even worship, draws part of its power from an awareness that we are in the presence of something almost divine.

Though we may smile at the infatuated couple, knowing that their current fascination with each other is probably only temporary, we should not totally discount what they are doing or feeling. The *Song of Solomon*, as well as other passages in

---

9   John 4:24.

the Scriptures (such as Psalm 45), validate at least some of their wonder and delight in each other. They are catching a glimpse of the loveliness of God himself. Maybe we should learn something from them, even as we pray that when they wake up, the hangover will not be too painful. This delight in another we often believe to be love itself, but as we shall see, love is so much more. With the correct definition of love, we can avoid a great deal of unnecessary disappointment, disagreements, and even divorce.

One Flesh

Desire: Delight engenders a desire to be with the other person. Distance frustrates us. We want to be close and to have uninterrupted communication. Soon, we also long for physical intimacy, beginning with a simple touch, holding hands, hugs, and then more and more. This desire is basically self-oriented, though it isn't necessarily selfish. We are seeking now to satisfy our own inward longing to possess and enjoy the other person, primarily for our own sake.

A few years ago, a Southern governor deserted his post for seven days to rendezvous with his lover in Argentina. His former supporters, the state's population, and his family were all devastated. Ironically, he had cited the requirement that a political leader must have "moral legitimacy" when President Bill Clinton was being charged with perjury and other crimes, some of them connected with his sordid sexual exploitation of a White House intern. Clinton had other affairs, too, but not nearly as many as John F. Kennedy, who apparently copulated with hundreds of women while in office. Both of these men imitated, but far exceeded, their famous presidential predecessors in adultery, Woodrow Wilson and F.D. Roosevelt. Nor are these holders of high executive office alone in their destructive dalliances. Famous preachers have ruined their ministries, and their marriages, by hooking up with other women, even as they decried the sins of fornication and adultery. We know all of this, but how shall we explain it?

Does animal passion alone drive a man to risk everything he holds dear? The dean of a major medical school once said to me, "I don't think anyone really appreciates the power of testosterone."[10] Indeed, this potent hormone impels men not only towards sexual gratification but also into restless activity of all sorts, including athletics, politics, business, and even Christian ministry. Of course, women are also tempted to extra-marital sexual relationships. On the other hand, though many commit adultery, not all do. And though there are plenty of attractive women in America, the governor mentioned above flew all the way to South America to link up with his Latin honey. What was so special about *her*? I am guessing that she seemed to fulfill other hungers than merely physical desire, and am almost certain that she offered him a kind of intimacy that he craved with all his heart and that perhaps, for whatever reason, he was not finding with his wife (though I do not for a moment blame her for his actions).

Genesis 2:18–25 describes the creation of the first man, Adam, and the formation from his body of the first woman, Eve. The passage begins with the flat statement of God himself, "'*It is* not good that man should be alone,'" and ends with these words: "Therefore a man shall leave his father and mother and be joined [cling; cleave] to his wife, and they shall become one flesh. And they were both naked, the man and his wife, and were not ashamed"[11] Loneliness; leaving the closest people in your life (your parents); cleaving to a woman; being naked and not ashamed. All of these are summed up in the phrase, "one flesh."

Men and women who violate the laws of God and society to engage in physical intimacy do so not only under the impulse of insistent bodily appetites, but also because they are seeking that original union and communion that characterized the first married couple. The depths of their soul cry out for the most profound intimacy possible, engaging body, mind, and heart; what we often call "love." Marriage is important, then, not only because it reflects the character of God, but because it enables us to express that which makes us human. We see not only our Maker in the other,

---

10 He was saying why he approved of my frank discussion of sexuality in the book, *The Lord's healing Words*, for which he kindly wrote a forward.

11 Gen 2:18, 24–25.

but also ourselves, our "other half," the one without whom we feel incomplete.

Sex and the Self

So, "God created man in his *own* image; in the image of God he created him; male and female he created them. Then God blessed them, and God said to them, 'Be fruitful and multiply; fill the earth and subdue it; have dominion over...every living thing that moves on the earth.'"[12] Marriage has great value because it reflects the being of the Triune God and expresses the fundamental unity-in-community of human nature itself. Furthermore, God meant for marriage to fulfill the deepest significance of our sexuality. Sex and the self are inseparable. You are either male or female, and this sexual identity extends to your very genes, affecting virtually everything you think and say and feel and do. From that standpoint, "biology is destiny." Though men and women share a common humanity, as created in God's image, we do so with a profound and ineradicable difference. God created Adam and Eve as sexual beings, and immediately gave them a mission that flowed from their unique gender roles: Together, they were to bear children, fill the earth, and exercise dominion over the world and all living creatures. Neither could do this alone. They must cooperate at every stage of this endeavor, and must do so out of their sexuality.

From another standpoint, therefore, we must affirm that biology is *not* destiny. The word "dominion" implies that those who rule the world can also rule themselves. In fact, the entire Bible, and especially the New Testament, assumes that we are unlike the animals in many ways, one of them being our ability to control our bodily passions. Contrary to the teachings of Freud and other materialists, we are not slaves to our sexuality. Marriage enables men and women to demonstrate their dominion over their own bodies (even as they submit to each other) by exercising self-control. Indeed, without mastery of one's sexual drives, mutually satisfying marital relations are impossible. Despite the power of sexual attraction, it can be tamed by a mind that rules the will. For

---

12   Gen 1:27–28.

this reason, all sexual actions that are not directed towards God's goal for marriage are both wrong and unnecessary. God has given us dominion over our own bodies so that we may seek to give rather than to get, to express love rather than to exploit another for one's own pleasure. This is only one reason why premarital sexual intimacy and any intimate relations with someone other than your own spouse bring (or ought to bring) such a sense of shame, guilt, and loss of dignity.

Sex and the self cannot be separated; sex and marriage are likewise inseparable. Thus, marriage connects us to, and allows us to fulfill, a fundamental aspect of our deepest essence as human beings. Sex is not only good, but, according to the Bible, "very good," in God's eyes.[13] This is only the case, however, when our sexuality builds, and flows from, married love and commitment. While love begins with *delight*, which leads to *desire*, it will die without *devotion*, and there is no better place to see this true love than in God himself.

Devotion: God and His People

Not only does marriage reflect God's nature, which is our essential being as humans, it also portrays the relationship of God to his people. Often in the Old Testament, Yahweh calls himself the Husband of Israel, the special nation that he chose to love. He is jealous for the undivided devotion of his chosen people, precisely because he has committed himself to an eternal covenant of love towards them.[14]

The entire book of Hosea depicts a God who will not let his wayward people go, even though they have proven themselves to be unfaithful by worshiping false gods. This departing from the one true God is called "harlotry,"[15] because the children of Abraham have been "wedded" to Yahweh by his promises to them. Nevertheless, after a time of painful discipline, God will receive them back to himself, and declares that Israel will again "call Me 'My Husband.'"[16]

---

13   Gen 1:31.
14   Ex 20:5; 34:14; Deut 24; etc.
15   Hos 1:2.
16   Hos 2:16.

God's intense love for his people also comes out in Ezekiel, where Yahweh declares, "I was crushed by their adulterous heart which has departed from Me, and by their eyes which play the harlot after their idols."[17] Speaking through the prophet, the Lord later describes how he found this people abandoned in the wilderness; how he washed and clothed them and adorned them like a beautiful bride; and how he entered into a covenant with them, and they became exclusively his.[18] Thus, Israel's lusting after idols evinces an ungrateful heart that both saddens and enrages her Maker and Savior. Many other passages could be cited.

When we come to the New Testament, John the Baptist calls himself the "friend"—comparable to the "best man" in our weddings today—and Jesus the "bridegroom,"[19] in clear allusion to these Old Testament pictures of God as the husband of his people. Jesus himself told parables about wedding feasts, in which God the Father is the King who gives a party for his Son, the bridegroom,[20] and he represents the groom who will come quickly for his bride.[21]

Paul declares that believers in Christ are no longer "married" to the law of God, but to Christ;[22] that he has "betrothed" them to Christ;[23] and that Christ is the Head of his body, the church, in an intimate relationship that is compared to that of husband and wife.[24] This analogy of marriage to depict the bond between God and his people centers upon God's saving love and actions. In other words, marriage not only portrays the nature of God as Maker and mankind as those created by him, but God as Savior and his people as those who have been rescued by him.

This means that the union of husband and wife is meant to display the love of a holy God for sinful men and women, and the grateful and loyal response that we owe to him. Both sides

---

17 Ez 6:9.
18 Ez 16:1–8.
19 John 3:29.
20 Mat 22:2–14.
21 Mat 25:1–13.
22 Rom 7:4.
23 2 Cor 11:2.
24 Eph 5:22–33.

of salvation are involved here: God's action and our expected response. This analogy does not signify some kind of spiritual superiority on the part of the man, but rather shows the kind of sacrificial love a man should have for his wife, and how he should pursue her spiritual growth; likewise, wives should show respect for their husbands the way the church responds to Christ. When men and women display this kind of relationship and forsake all others and cling loyally to each other, the marvelous, unconditional love of God for wicked sinners and the corresponding love of the saved for their Savior are put on display for all the world to see. As Timothy Keller writes, "marriage was designed to be a reflection of the saving love of God for us in Jesus Christ.. That is why the gospel helps us to understand marriage and marriage helps us to understand the gospel."[25]

The Scriptural Importance of Marriage

The relationship between man and woman is mentioned so often in the Bible, and at so many key points, that it forms a major theme of God's revelation. As we have seen, creation of man and woman as husband and wife comes in the first two chapters of the Bible. The disruption of their relationship follows in chapter three of Genesis, followed by the largely negative examples of Abraham and Sarah; Isaac and Rebecca (in their later years); Jacob and his wives; Samson and Delilah; David's plural marriages; the multiple wives of Solomon, which destroyed him; and other examples in the historical books of the Old Testament.

The laws given by God through Moses prominently feature marriage or matters intimately related to it. Two of the Ten Commandments—"Honor your father and your mother" and "You shall not commit adultery"—plant marriage firmly into God's moral framework. The last commandment—"You shall not covet"—explicitly refers to discontent in marriage and implicitly forbids lust, while the prohibition against taking the Lord's name in vain reminds us of the sanctity of the marriage vow. Other laws regulate sexual activity and describe what is lawful and what

---

25 Keller, *The Meaning of Marriage*, 8.

violates God's holy will for the relationship between the sexes.[26]

Likewise, the wisdom, poetical, and prophetic literature highlight the importance of marriage. We have the many warnings about going after a "strange woman" in Proverbs, balanced by the lovely statements about happiness in marriage and the assertion that he who finds a wife finds a good thing, and similar evaluations.[27] In Ecclesiastes, Solomon advises a man to enjoy life with his wife.[28] The Psalms contain a beautiful wedding song.[29] The prophetic books often employ the metaphor of Israel as wife of her savior, Yahweh, as we have noted before. The entire book of Hosea is built on this theme, but Isaiah, Jeremiah, and Ezekiel pick up on it, portraying Israel's idolatry as spiritual adultery, and Yahweh as her faithful husband.[30]

We have noted that Jesus told parables about marriage; John the Baptist called Jesus the Bridegroom and himself the friend of the bride; and Paul refers several times to the church as the bride of Christ. We find instructions for married life, as well as the high importance of marriage, in 1 Peter and Hebrews, along with prohibitions against fornication and adultery in other epistles. The last book of the Bible concludes with a glorious picture of a church that is prepared like a bride for her husband to convey something of the beauty and wonder of our final and eternal union with Christ in the New Heaven and the New Earth.[31] We should not ignore the prohibitions of divorce and remarriage after divorce which fell from the lips of Jesus contained in all three Synoptic Gospels.[32]

Can anyone, after reflecting even a moment on the prominent place of the male-female relationship, of which marriage

---

26 Ex 20:1–17; Lev 19:20–22, 29–30; 20:10–21; Deut 5:1–21.
27 Prov 5:18; 31:10 ff; 12:4; 18:22; 19:14.
28 Eccl 9:9.
29 Ps 45.
30 See, for example, Isa 54:5; 62:4–5; Jer 3:14; Ez 6:7; 16:1–63; Hos 2:19–23.
31 Mat 9: 15; 25:1–13; Mk 2:19–20; Lk 5:34–35; John 3:29; Rom 7:1–6; 1 Cor 7:1–40; Eph 5:22–33; Col 3:18–19; Heb 13:4; 1 Pet 3:1–7; Rev 19:7, 8; 21:2,9; 22:17; etc.
32 Mat 5:31–32; 19:1–9; Mk 10:1–12; Lk 16:18. See my articles on this subject at www.chinainst.org.

forms the central example, ever again discount the immense value of the marital bond? Do not these repeated references, at crucial points in all portions of Scripture, impress upon us the necessity of promoting, preserving, and protecting the union of man and wife?

Recipients of Revelation

Now let us think about God's original plan for marriage, and what it means for us today. We shall begin with a fundamental truth: The first thing that God did after creating Adam and Eve was to speak to them. Being created in the image of God, the man and the woman could understand his words. Before all time, the triune God was a communicating society of Father, Son, and Holy Spirit. "In the beginning was the Word, and the Word was with God."[33] Words belong to the fundamental nature of God, and thus must constitute a basic element in the image in which he created man and woman.

Despite being finite and limited, Adam and Eve were recipients of divine revelation from the very beginning of their life on earth. Those who say that creatures cannot understand their Creator, or that language cannot convey exact truth about God, are wrong. Otherwise, what does Genesis mean when it records God's words to Adam and Eve? "Then God blessed them, and God said to them, 'Be fruitful and multiply; fill the earth and subdue it.'"[34]

God's plan for married couples, then, begins with his intention to speak to them. He means for his word to dwell among them richly, for them to teach and admonish one another, speaking the truth in love.[35] Adam and Eve, as recipients of God's revelation, were to keep these words in their hearts and then pass on what they had heard to the children whom the Lord commanded them

---

33 John 1:1.
34 Gen 1:28. We must distinguish between God's incomprehensibility, which means that we can never know all about him, and his alleged ineffability, which says that we can't know or say anything that exactly corresponds to God's nature. The former is true; the latter is refuted by every page of the Bible.
35 Col 3:16; Eph 4:15.

to bear in abundance, just as Moses commanded later Israelites.[36] The origin of marriage is God's word to himself, "Let Us make man in Our image,"[37] and the first marriage commenced with the man and the woman hearing God's word of blessing and command.

Male and Female

"In the image of God he created him; male and female he created them."[38] Men and women, while both being made in the image of God, reflect that image differently. They share common traits that are fundamental to human nature, but they also possess distinctive characteristics that mark them as male or female. These differences are hinted at in the Bible and intuitively perceived by people of all eras, cultures, and races. Various fields of study, including psychology, sociology, and physiology, provide abundant evidence that these differences are universal; they are, in other words, "hard-wired."[39] The hormones testosterone and estrogen affect all of the body's systems, and significantly different levels of them in men and women lead to markedly different outlooks and activities. Psychological and social distinctives reflect both our creation in the image of God and our fallen nature, and cannot be completely assigned either to one or the other, since we now have no experience of moral perfection.

Before mentioning some of these, we need to understand that they are relative, for each sex shares most of these traits with the other sex, with some men being more "feminine" (not effeminate) and some women being more "masculine" (not mannish) than others of their same gender. They are relative also in that they apply only when men and women are being compared. These distinctions are also morally neutral; rather than assigning moral values to the differences, we should merely state them as

---

36   Deut 6:6–9.
37   Gen 1:26.
38   Gen 1:27.
39   Resources for the following section include Clark, *Man and Woman*, 371-448; Johnson, "The Biological Basis for Gender-specific Behavior," 280–93; Harley, *His Needs, Her Needs*; Gray, *Men Are from Mars, Women Are from Venus*.

observed realities, and respect the value of each gender equally. Individual personality traits make some generalizations invalid for some people. The distinctions lie in the realms of psychological structure and social behavior; they do not involve intelligence, skill, or ability. The "negative" traits (such as aggressiveness in men) should be controlled at times, rather than encouraged, for we live in a fallen world. That having been said, we should be aware of, and honor, some very basic and marked differences that greatly affect our married life.

In general, women tend to share common features. They are more holistic and integrated in body, mind, and emotions. The female central nervous system is much more interconnected than the male's; women are thus are more capable of receiving and processing sensory nerve input. They are more perceptive of their environment and have finer senses of touch, hearing, smell, taste, and color, and can tolerate brighter lights. They have greater ability to perform multiple tasks at the same time. Women's hormonal rhythm is more cyclical than that of men. They have a thicker layer of fat under their skin, which enables them to endure cold better and to have energy for tasks requiring unusual endurance.[40] They need to eat more to maintain necessary nutrients, which makes them more liable to gaining unwanted weight. They also mature more quickly, are more resistant to infectious disease, and live longer.

Women are more alert socially, as they are more perceptive of their own and others' emotional states. They can integrate what they sense and remember more easily, and form a much more balanced and well-rounded impression of a personal encounter than men can. They tend to have greater verbal ability and drive, needing to speak at least 11,000 words per day to feel comfortable (whereas men only need to speak 5,000 words).[41] They tend to be

---

40 See   http://theconversation.com/why-men-and-women-cant-agree-on-the-perfect-temperature-66585.

41 See http://time.com/4837536/do-women-really-talk-more/ ; http://time.com/4837536/do-women-really-talk-more/
Although this seems to depend on context. See https://www.hsph.harvard.edu/news/features/do-women-talk-more-than-men/

more patient, compliant, empathetic, and nurturing, especially of their own children, to whose needs they are naturally responsive. They are quicker to be intimate with new acquaintances.[42] Women communicate to establish or strengthen a relationship; when a woman imparts information, she wants to draw another closer to herself. For women, "no news is bad news"; they desire repeated verbal expressions of affirmation and affection. "If you are not praising me, you are unhappy with me." When a woman is upset, she wants to talk it out in order to express herself, be understood, and get a sympathetic hearing.[43]

Men, on the other hand, share other traits. They tend to be more aggressive, assertive, physical, action-oriented, and reactive. They have a stronger drive for power, wealth, fame, and resources. Their brains enable them to separate sensory and thinking processes into compartments, allowing for quicker responses to important stimuli. This may explain their greater affinity for categorical thinking. The male brain tends to be more "single-minded, focused, less distracted, and perhaps less socially aware. This coupled with the hot-wired limbic system may increase males' competitive, goal-setting, rule-making, and hierarchical approach to social interaction."[44] They are more emotionally stable and constant and tend to be full of self-confidence (even pride, presumption, and arrogance). Men are generally bigger and their circulatory system makes them able to build more muscle and perform heavy work. Men also tend to have better hand and eye coordination and possess better night vision. Less stimulation is required for men to respond to food, sexual, or threat stimuli. They are quicker to act and make decisions and are less bothered by conflict. They are more object- and product-oriented; what matters is the outcome, the "bottom line."

Men approach interaction with others differently. Rather than more intimate relationships, they are more likely to form

---

42 Johnson, "The Biological Basis for Gender-specific Behavior," 281.
43 John Gray, Men Are from Mars, Women Are from Venus.
44 Johnson, "The Biological Basis for Gender-specific Behavior," 289–90.

larger groups.[45] For men, communication is more for the exchange of information rather than for building relationships. The focus is on solving a problem or achieving a goal. Men dislike repetition, seeing it as a waste of time once something has been said once. For men, "No news is good news"; they enjoy verbal affirmation, but assume that, "if you are not criticizing me, you are happy with me." If a man is upset, he will first tend to isolate himself in order to figure out how to solve the problem, then sometimes seek out someone he considers to be an "expert" and ask for advice.[46]

Differing Desires

Just as men and women exhibit different characteristics, they also generally have differing desires. Christian psychologist and marriage counselor Willard Harley discusses these in his book, *His Needs, Her Needs*[47] According to Harley, the five most important things for a wife are: affection (non-sexual expressions of care and concern); conversation (consisting mostly of how she feels about her life, and how he feels about how she feels, though including some about how he is doing); openness and honesty that allow her to trust him completely; financial support and security; and family commitment (she wants him to be a good father). Men, on the other hand, have a different set of expectations: sex ("the one thing he can't do without"); recreational companionship; an attractive spouse; domestic support (he wants a home that is peaceful and well-ordered); and admiration and respect from his wife.

Dr. Emerson Eggerichs sums up these differences in his book *Love and Respect* by saying that a wife wants more than anything else to be loved, while a husband desires respect first and foremost.[48] He bases this on Ephesians 5:22–33 and spells it out further with two acronyms, COUPLE and CHAIRS. The wife

---

45 Johnson, "The Biological Basis for Gender-specific Behavior," 281.
46 John Gray, *Men Are from Mars, Women Are from Venus*.
47 Harley, *His Needs, Her Needs*
48 Emerson Eggerichs, *Love & Respect: The Love She Most Desires, The Respect He Desperately Needs* (Nashville: Thomas Nelson, 2004). This is one of the most helpful books about marriage I have ever read.

wants: Closeness; Openness (as in "opening up"); Understanding (not "fixing," just listening); Peacemaking (say, "I'm sorry"); Loyalty; Esteem (honor and cherish). The husband, on the other hand, longs for his wife to appreciate his drives toward Conquest (work and achieve); Hierarchy (protect and provide); Authority (serve and lead); Insight (analyze and counsel); Relationship (shoulder-to-shoulder friendship); and Sexuality.

We should note also that men and women seem to "fall in love" a bit differently. Comparatively speaking, men are "turned on" by physical appearance and closeness, whereas for women, affectionate, caring words evoke a strong response. These differences, though real, do not mean that each sex doesn't appreciate, and perhaps deeply want, what the other does. For example, women have a strong sexual drive also, and are attracted to good-looking men. But it's the relative proportion and importance of these drives that make us so unlike each other, and so complementary to each other. Remember, both are equally created in the image of God, and carry his likeness, even in our current fallen state.

Companionship

"And the LORD God said, '*It is* not good that man should be alone; I will make him a helper comparable to him' ... And the LORD God caused a deep sleep to fall on Adam, and he slept; and he took one of his ribs, and closed up the flesh in its place. Then the rib which the LORD God had taken from man he made into a woman, and he brought her to the man. And Adam said

> '*This is now bone of my bones*
> *And flesh of my flesh;*
> *She shall be called Woman,*
> *Because she was taken out of Man.*'"[49]

One of the reasons that older single men die sooner than they "should" is that they are lonely. If you want to break a man, put him into solitary confinement. Unattached people congregate

---

49 Gen 2:18, 21–23.

in singles' bars and clubs seeking a companion. We are not meant to live alone. Remember that we are created in God's image, and that this God is an eternal society of Father, Son, and Spirit. Thus, the desire for companionship is rooted in our DNA, buried deep in our souls, and testified by much of our anatomy—eyes that make contact, ears that listen, lips that speak and kiss, hands that hold, hearts that beat with affection and concern, and much more. So, what marks marital companionship?

Man and wife share a common life. They live, eat, work, and sleep together. Their sexual intimacy joins them into a union that the Bible repeatedly terms "one flesh."[50] As Adam put it, Eve was to him "bone of my bones and flesh of my flesh." That is why the death of a spouse produces the same sort of grief that loss of a major limb inflicts upon us. Husband and wife share something so deep that no one can explain but that we must honor and preserve. No wonder Jesus was so adamantly opposed to divorce![51]

Not only a shared physical life, but shared thoughts and words bind man and wife to each other. Because they live together, married people have the opportunity speak to each other at different times of the day—and they should! As Father, Son, and Holy Spirit engaged in a holy conversation to bring men and women into existence ("Let Us make man in Our image"[52]), so honest, loving speech forms the lifeblood of any marriage that would correspond to God's initial intention. Studies have shown that communication is the *sine qua non* (the one thing that can't be absent) of a healthy marital relationship. It is true that some people are more talkative than others, and that women tend to express themselves verbally more than men do, but all married people must open their minds and hearts to each other, in an attitude of mutual respect and acceptance, in order for their union to grow and deepen.

Theirs is a common mission: to be fruitful and multiply, to fill the earth, to reflect God's glory in all they do. With different

---

50   Gen 2:24; Mar 10:8; Eph 5:31.
51   Mat 5:32; 19:9; Mar 10:11; Lk 16:18.
52   Gen 1:26.

anatomies and personalities, husband and wife will fulfill their individual destinies distinctively, but they should do so in close collaboration with each other. Cooperation, not competition, will enable them to complete the tasks God has assigned to them. To the greatest extent possible, married people need to plan together, asking God for wisdom about how they can best serve him as a unit, not as two discrete actors on different stages. They will of necessity play different roles, but they should do so in the same drama, with the same script, under the same divine Director, and for the same audience. Today's notion of "space" was not concocted in heaven, but in a world where individual, ego-centered, personal actualization dominates discussions about happiness. In an age of profound and pervasive loneliness, a God-centered marriage can mirror divine community by building a companionship that grows richer by the day.

For these and other reasons, Timothy Keller cites research that proves that "**most people are happy in their marriages, and most of those who are not and who don't get divorced eventually become happy.**"[53] I emphasize those words because, when God said that the creation of man and woman in his image was "very good," he knew what he was saying![54] A "happy" marriage is possible, despite perceptions to the contrary.

Leaving Parents

"Therefore a man shall leave his father and mother and be joined to his wife, and they shall become one flesh."[55]

Because the woman was taken from the man, and is "bone of [his] bones and flesh of [his] flesh,"[56] their descendants would likewise leave their parents in order to be joined to a spouse. That is, marriage between a man and a woman constitutes a closer bond than even the parent-child relationship. Fathers and mothers often find this fact difficult to accept, but it stands as a fundamental reality that cannot be denied. For this reason, a healthy marriage

---

53   Keller, *The Meaning of Marriage*, 19.
54   Gen 1:31.
55   Gen 2:24.
56   Gen 2:23.

demands that husband and wife "leave" their parents and "cleave" to each other. The man, in particular, must be willing to break the bond of dependence upon his father and mother, and especially his close emotional ties to his mother, in order to from an even closer union with his wife.

This leaving does not absolve children from the duty to honor their parents, expressed so clearly in many parts of the Bible,[57] but it does erect boundaries on the limit of obedience and emotional closeness to parents after one marries. From now on, the most important person in married persons' life is not their father or mother, but their husband or wife. What does it mean to "leave"? First, physical separation must take place. At the very least, this requires not living under the same roof or using the same kitchen. Implied in this physical departure is the concept of a change in authority. The young couple must set up their own household, of which the husband is the head,[58] not his father, and certainly not his mother. Responsibility for the nurture and care of his wife and children must rest primarily upon the husband, not upon his parents; the same goes for teaching and ruling his children.

Likewise, a wife needs to be mistress of her own household, under her husband's leadership and protection, and not subject to her mother, mother-in-law or other women. Otherwise, how can she fulfill her mandate to love her husband and children, submitting to him alone (under God) and expecting them to honor and obey her as they do their father?[59] Though we are to honor our elders, obedience is due primarily to our parents (when we are young). That implies that they, and not anyone else, even our grandparents, have authority over the home.

Loving Leadership

God's original design for marriage calls for the husband to serve his wife as a loving leader, and for her to submit to him as a

---

57 E.g., Ex 20:12; Eph 6:1–3.
58 Eph 5:22–23,
59 See Eph 5:22–24; 1 Tim 5:9-10, 14; Tit 2:4-5.

suitable helper. In today's climate, such a comment will surely spark controversy, since it might seem to smack of male dominance and exploitation of women, but that is not the case. The Bible nowhere condones male domination or a dismissive, condescending posture towards women; just the reverse. Created in the image of God, women are equal to men in intrinsic value, just as they possess attributes common to men, such as intelligence, compassion, and the like. God commands all people in positions of authority to care for those for whose welfare they are responsible. Jesus explicitly told his disciples that they are not to lord it over one another, but to imitate his example of sacrificial service,[60] and Paul commands husbands to love their wives "as Christ also loved the church and gave Himself for her."[61]

At the same time, however, we must recognize that the biblical pattern for marriage frankly includes male leadership. Consider: Adam was created first, a fact that Paul draws upon later.[62] Eve was created to be a companion and helper to Adam;[63] as Paul writes, "Nor was man created for the woman, but woman for the man."[64] Just as he had named the animals that were brought to him, so Adam named his newly-fashioned helper.[65] Even after the Fall, he bestowed upon her another name, "Eve," "because she was the mother of all living [people]."[66] In the Bible, conferring a name upon someone assumes that the person named is in some way subordinate to the one giving the name.

Even in the New Testament, where all believers are equally "in Christ," a husband is called "the head" of his wife, as Christ is the "head" of the church, and this relationship is further defined as one of leadership and submission.[67] Men are to provide for and

---

60 Matt 20:25–38.
61 Eph 5:25.
62 Gen 2:7, 18–22; 1 Tim 2:13.
63 Gen 2:18.
64 1 Cor 11:9.
65 Gen 2:19–20, 23.
66 Gen 3:20.
67 Eph 5:22–32; see also Eph 1:20–23; Col 3:18; Tit 2:5.

protect their women.[68] Furthermore, most men thoroughly enjoy this role. They want to be "heroes" and to care for their wives. Men are willing to die for the women under their care; they see this as a matter of honor. So, women can choose to fight this God-given order and resist male authority, or they can make friends with it, and allow their men to develop compassion, kindness, and tenderness.

A Suitable Helper

"And the LORD God said, 'It is not good that man should be alone; I will make him a helper comparable to him.'"[69]

Eve was formed as a helper suitable for Adam, a soul companion with whom he could share his heart and an indispensable colleague in his life's mission. As we have seen, that mission includes bearing and bringing up children, and then, with their children, ruling the earth on God's behalf. Lest we think that this section from the first book of the Bible has nothing to do with us today, in this fallen world and under the New Covenant, the Apostle Paul reiterates the point: "Nor was man created for the woman, but woman for the man."[70] Of course, he goes on to emphasize the mutuality of the male-female relationship by saying, "Nevertheless, neither is man independent of woman, nor woman independent of man, in the Lord. For as the woman came from man, even so man also comes through woman; but all things are from God."[71]

Contrary to ideas that are almost universally accepted today, the Bible teaches that a wife's primary role is to be a helper and companion ("comparable to") her husband. She does not lose her identity in this position, but rather fulfills the purpose for which she was created. With her own personality and possessing equal worth (she is created in the image of God just as he is), a married woman actualizes her full potential by enabling her husband to serve God in the particular way that God has ordained. We see here

68   Eph 5:28-29.
69   Gen 2:18.
70   1 Cor 11:9.
71   1 Cor 11:11–12.

how much a husband needs his wife! Proud men may ignore this fact, but only to their peril and great loss. Fashioned in the image of God, with intelligence and value no less than his, she brings unique perspective, sensitivity, and skills to their relationship and common task.[72]

It follows that women who are looking to build their own separate career, independent of that of their husbands, and who do not see marriage and motherhood (if God grants children) as their primary sphere of worth and work, may want to consider whether they should get married. In our society, they have freedom to pursue their ambitions and dreams, and may do so if they think God is leading them in that direction. But if they desire to be married, those aspirations must be subordinated, and often even sacrificed, to the demands of providing their husbands with the friendship and help they so desperately need, and their children with the love that only a mother can give.

My father, who had a very successful and extremely demanding career in the Navy, often said to me, "I have come this far because I never had to worry about what was happening at home, for your mother always did her part well." This is not to deny the husband's duty to help out at home, and even to take the lead, but just to emphasize the immeasurable contribution to her own family and to society that a faithful wife and mother can make.

"More Precious than Rubies"

"Who can find a virtuous wife [Lit. *a wife of valor*, in the sense of all forms of excellence]? For her worth *is* far above rubies. The heart of her husband safely trusts her; so he will have no lack of gain. She does him good and not evil all the days of her life... Charm *is* deceitful and beauty *is* passing, but a woman *who* fears the LORD, she shall be praised. Give her the fruit of her hands, and let her own works praise her in the gates."[73]

Proverbs 31:10–31 paints a picture of a truly amazing

---

72 See especially Prov 31:10-31.
73 Prov 31:10–12, 26–37.

woman. This wife possesses a remarkable array of competencies, so much so that she might be a composite picture, an ideal that no one wife could fulfill. She gathers fiber and makes it into clothing for her family, selling the surplus to generate income. No sluggard, she is up before dawn to make sure that all the members of her household have plenty to eat. Perhaps as she goes to market, she notices a piece of property and buys it, turning it into a profitable vineyard. Her business acumen and the garments she fashions bring honor to her husband, enabling him to become a leader in the community. She is both strong and honorable, with a profound joy based on faith in God, which she expresses with words of wisdom and kindness to other women and their children.

A wife can provide her husband with healthy food; a quiet and peaceful home; advice, encouragement, and prayer; physical affection; a more playful spirit that relieves his masculine tendency to be too serious; social skills that he lacks; stimulation to build friendships with others; nurture and care for the children while he is gone; and a lovely face and figure to satisfy his longing for feminine beauty. The reward for her constant diligence comes as praise from her family, for in all her activity she has not neglected them. She has worked *from* her home, not away from her home, so that they have only commendation for this woman of surpassing excellence.

Clearly, the root cause of all this consists in her reverence towards God. She is a God-fearing woman, meaning that she trusts him, loves him, and seeks to obey him. Created in the image of her Maker, she responds to him with cheerful obedience. Only this sort of companion can match the needs of her husband, who must have someone with whom he can share his own love for God and sense of mission from God. The passage ends with an exhortation even more needed now than when it was written: Give this woman her due praise! She has more than physical beauty; she possesses a beautiful soul and lives a beautiful life. How different from the values of our society!

In recent decades, a tremendous shift has come over marriage in almost all developed nations. Wives are expected to work outside the home in jobs that are usually not related to their husbands' jobs. Economic necessity often compels wives to work outside the home, many men now expect their wives to provide at least half the family income, and many women aspire to a successful career that has nothing to do with their husband's career. Some Christian women also believe that God has given them gifts that should be used to advance the Lord's purposes in the world and in the church. Though each couple must make this decision for themselves, we should face a hard truth: Most women are not able both to fulfill their responsibilities to their husbands and to their children and to devote themselves fully to a career. Usually, the husband and children suffer from the neglect that necessarily follows from the woman's limited time and energy for home after she has given so much at work. Some couples can succeed in this balancing act, but most do not.

When a wife really has to work outside her home, therefore, adjustments will have to be made so that she can have as much time and energy free as possible for her husband, her children, her own physical health (including rest and exercise), and her housework. To make this possible, husbands will have to sacrifice.

For a longer treatment of the incalculable value of a godly wife, see my little book, *More Precious than Rubies*. http://www.reachingchineseworldwide.org/more-precious-than-rubies

Children

The first word that the Lord addressed to the first newly-married couple was one of blessing. "Then God blessed them, and God said to them, 'Be fruitful and multiply; fill the earth and subdue it.'"[74] From this we learn that marriage is a blessed condition, not a burden or bondage, as so many believe today. Let us note at the beginning how God himself defines the blessedness of marriage. "Be fruitful and multiply." That is, have children, lots of them!

These words sound strange to us today, with the background of fears of population growth outstripping the ability of the earth to sustain so many people, and of unwanted children straining

---

74   Gen 1:28.

the resources of an exhausted, poor, or even unmarried couple. Although much could be said to address these concerns, let us here simply reflect on this clear declaration of God's original design for marriage. Marriage is meant to produce children: offspring, progeny, fellow-bearers of the image of God. The Creator likes the reflection of himself which he calls man (which includes male and female), and he wants more of them. He pronounces this final act of creation, including the formation of man and woman to be sexual, reproducing representations of his very nature—to be "very good."[75]

We can confidently conclude, therefore, that the union of man and woman in matrimony should include from the beginning the expectation that children will issue from their intimate relations, and that these children will be welcomed as gifts from God. "Behold, children *are* a heritage from the LORD, the fruit of the womb *is* a reward."[76] Everywhere in Scripture, the birth of children is hailed as a great blessing, and barrenness is bewailed as a terrible bane. A marriage that does not produce children does not conform to the original plan. In this fallen world, many factors, including fertility, can result in childlessness, but we should strongly affirm the goodness of having children, and the fundamental place that producing offspring holds in the very nature and purpose of marriage.

Why might this be the case? Consider first that children testify to the unique biological features of men and women as male and female. They prove that their parents have, at least once, enjoyed the one-flesh communion of the marriage act of which Scripture speaks so often and so approvingly. When a man and woman become parents, their love for each other expands into a mutual affection for the little person who combines their characteristics and reminds them of each other, and extends beyond mutual care for each other into a common love for another. Both father and mother grow into greater maturity as they shoulder the demands of bringing up children, thereby learning and expressing

---

75 Gen 1:31.
76 Ps 127:3.

more of what it means to be created in the image of God. The same can be said of adoption, in which we can be imitators of God, who adopted us as his dearly beloved children.

The coming of a child into the world allows a woman to nurse and nurture her little one; her breasts then not only give delight to her husband,[77] but also provide life-giving nourishment for her baby. Speaking very concretely but also very reverently, we may say that the parts of the body that afford the greatest pleasure engender a living being whose very existence—not to mention the manifold joys that a child brings to his parents—gives constant token of their love for each other in the image of God the Father. For this reason, to marry without meaning to have children constitutes a violation of God's revealed will, unless there are highly compelling reasons dictating such a choice. Likewise, to engage in sexual relations outside of marriage ignores, and even blasphemes, part of the purpose for our sexuality. Children born out of wedlock are still gifts of God, but are innocent sufferers of wanton selfishness and folly. (Of course, children resulting from rape testify to the wicked power of lust in men, and not necessarily to the folly of the woman, unless she unwisely placed herself in a situation where unwanted sexual activity would likely result.)

Christians disagree about whether measures should be taken to prevent conception. All Christian ethicists, however, should agree that using contraceptives should be decided upon with prayer and serious thought as to the considerations behind this choice and the possible consequences of not only the various methods but also the character of a relationship that does not conform to the natural pattern of life. If faith in God, love (including mutual consent), and hope are lacking, then such an action should be questioned. Some serious students of the Bible firmly believe that God's Word does not warrant any human intervention in the process of procreation. That is, with the Roman Catholics, they believe that birth control methods, unless the mother's health is at risk, are not in accordance with God's will. Pointing to previous generations, when women bore as many as a dozen children or

---

77 Prov 5:19.

more while engaging in very strenuous household tasks without the assistance of modern machines, they say that we should not think that women today are any less capable. To the argument that bringing up children and educating them in this modern age involves huge financial expense, they counter with many cases of families who have somehow managed to provide for large families, often through home education and home businesses, as well as college education scholarships. If we are trusting God and seeking to follow his way, God will supply all that we need, they affirm.

These Christians also remind us that the culture of birth control feeds our human tendency to assume we can take control of all aspects of our lives, including the birth of children, and they question whether we have sufficiently questioned many of the values, such as convenience and comfort, that have contributed to a cavalier attitude towards the God-mandated connection between sexual relations in marriage and the sub-creation of new life.

On the other hand, other equally godly people think that we must be flexible about such matters, especially when having a lot of children may impose a burden on others, including society, to care for them if the parents cannot. They refer to the Creation Mandate to "subdue" the earth and apply it also to "be fruitful and multiply," with the implication that we are also to exercise dominion over how many children we bring into the world.

In my opinion, regardless of which position we adopt, we all must acknowledge the vital role of children in the life of any healthy marriage, except where God chooses to withhold them.

Let us pause to ponder that great privilege of imitating God by enjoying such an intimate union in which new life is born!

Dominion

After telling Adam and Eve to multiply and fill the earth, the Lord commanded them and their posterity to "subdue it and have dominion over" every living creature.[78] Indeed, carrying the likeness of God includes having dominion over the other creatures,

---

78 Gen 1:28.

as Adam began to do when he conferred names on each sort of animal.[79] Like our Maker, we are meant to rule over the creation, not as creators or owners, but as faithful stewards of what belongs to God. This authority implies responsibility, of course, as Adam was put into the garden to tend it,[80] not to destroy God's beautiful handiwork. God's image-bearers are to care for the creation as his appointed guardians and managers, rather than as ravenous wolves.

What, then, does dominion have to do with marriage? A great deal, actually. Adam needed someone to help him carry out his mission. None of the animals possessed the required capacity to be a helper, suitable to the man, so the woman was formed out of him and presented to him.[81] Together, they received the mandate to subdue the earth, and only together can they fulfill their common mission. Husband and wife are meant to work together productively, along with their children, to manage the resources the Lord has given them.

Self-control enables us to exercise God-ordained rule, and is indeed required for such a role. Within marriage, we must exert control over our eyes, lips, ears, thoughts, appetites, time, and even our sexuality. As we have seen, some consider the use of birth control to be a means of stewarding our bodies. As we rule ourselves, we are equipped to keep our houses in order, so that money, possessions, and time are servants, not masters, of our combined life together. In other words, God's original plan called for married people to live ordered lives, managing themselves, children, and material possessions according to his revealed will. Even in the New Covenant, we see this command for personal self-control and sovereignty over our households as a requirement for church leadership.[82] Of course, authority can be abused in a fallen world, so the New Testament tempers its teaching on authority by emphasizing the responsibility to serve with humility.[83]

---

79 Gen 1:26.
80 Gen 2:15,
81 Gen 2:20–22.
82 1Tim 3:1–12.
83 Matt 20:25–28; Eph 5:25–32; 1 Tim 3:3.

What might household dominion look like? We may see it in a tidy house and yard; an orderly schedule; well-behaved children and animals; balanced checkbook and paid-up credit card; and temperance in speech, food, and entertainment. Let your imagination roam, and see what thoughts come to mind as you ponder the beauty of Adam and Eve working together in the Garden! And remember, God forgives repentant sinners!

CHAPTER TWO

THE BAD:
WHAT WE HAVE DONE
TO MARRIAGE

What has happened to this beautiful plan of God? As we all know, men and women are not living as God intended, and the awful consequences are all around us. True, some couples seem to bask in the glow of their first love throughout their life together, but they are in the minority. Usually, after a period of weeks or months, sometimes longer, the fires of infatuation are doused by the cold water of daily life together, and then quenched by the flood of disappointment and even despair that engulfs most couples. The other's faults and failings, not to mention what seems to be—and probably is—a radical change of behavior, even character, since the wedding day combine to dispel the mist that enveloped us in the warm embrace of romance. We thought that wine and roses would last forever, but they are driven out by vinegar and thorns.[84]

Perhaps nothing in life has the potential to evoke as much perplexity and pain as our fixation upon, and frustration with, the other sex. We are familiar with the litany of woes that now

---

84 You will encounter some repetition of material from the first chapter in the next two chapters, because I am following basically the same outline and also because some themes need to be repeated to make an impression on our minds.

attend the male-female relationship: arguments, estrangement, separation, abandonment, physical violence, divorce. Just listen to any country music station for a few minutes and you will hear both the ecstasy of "I have found my true love!" in one song and the agony of "I've lost my lover!" in the next. So, how do we understand this discrepancy between our expectations of marital bliss and our experience of something much less, something that perhaps even resembles torture?

God's Image Defaced

As we saw earlier, marriage has great value because it reflects the essential nature of the Triune God and expresses the fundamental unity-in-community of human nature itself. We fall in love partly because we discern in the other person something of God's own beauty and goodness. But we can also fall out of love very quickly when we discover that the person we married is not perfect! The Bible teaches that "all have sinned and fall short of the glory of God."[85] Though created to be like God, we have abandoned our true destiny and become rebels against our Maker. "There is no one that does good, no, not one."[86] This doesn't mean that we are all, always, as bad as we could be, but that we are all, always, not as good as we should be.

The root of our rebellion can be found in our refusal to orient our lives towards God. Though we are all aware that there must be a supreme being of eternal power and divine nature, we turn away from this awareness. We do not worship God as God, nor do we give thanks to him.[87] Instead, we fashion for ourselves substitute "gods"—idols that reflect something in creation. The most common of these fabrications is another person, and especially someone of the other sex.[88] Therefore, instead of seeing the other as created in the *image* of God, we treat him or her as God himself. Forgetting that he or she is a mere creature, we look for life, happiness, fulfillment, and satisfaction in another human.

---

85   Rom 3:23.
86   Rom 3:12.
87   Rom 1:21.
88   See Rom 1:18–23.

No wonder we are disappointed! Our mate is neither divine nor devoid of moral flaws. Far from it! Not only are we finite, and thus unable to fill the place in the heart that only God can occupy, but we are also fallen from our original goodness, and thus morally crippled and corrupt. Our inflated expectations turn into bitter disappointment, simply because we were "worshiping" something that cannot save or satisfy us. We can find unconditional acceptance in God, but not in another person. God alone can give us joy and happiness, for he only possesses the wisdom, power, and love to slake our thirst for profound peace and intimacy. If we would simply give up our unrealistic hopes for another human being to make us happy, we would save ourselves a great deal of heartache.

"The woman whom You gave *to be*[89] with me, she gave me of the tree, and I ate."[90] See Adam's radical change of heart! From delighting in Eve, he denounces her for tempting him into sin. At the same time, he denounces God for giving the woman to him. She is no longer a precious gift, but the occasion—note, *not* the cause, as he claims—of his rebellion against God and thus alienation from the source of all happiness. It is true that Eve gave Adam the forbidden fruit, but the sin of eating was his own, as Paul says.[91] He was intended to lead her as her head,[92] but he followed her instead. Clearly, his own love for God had given way to his focus upon Eve. Turning his eyes from the Lord, he looked upon his wife and the pleasures she was wrongly offering when she gave him the forbidden fruit. Shutting his ears to God's command, he heeded the voice of a woman. There is a proper love of a husband for his wife, and there is also a sinful subservience to her wishes.

Likewise, the erstwhile helper turned into a fatal hindrance. The gift became a curse. The delight of his eyes led to the destruction of his soul. By allowing herself to be deceived by

---

89 In the *New King James Version* of the Bible that is used here, words not in the original Hebrew or Greek but added for clarity of meaning are put into italics.

90 Gen 3:12.

91 Rom 5:12, 15.

92 Eph 5:23.

Satan, Eve abandoned her God and ruined her man. Insurrection against God's order would entail constant conflict between the former partners. How often we repeat this tragedy when we put sight before obedient faith![93]

Inevitably, idolatry breeds disdain, as we discover that our spouse is not a Greek god or goddess, much less God Almighty. The "knight in shining armor" turns out to be a regular guy—messy, forgetful, insensitive, and even a bit gross. The sweet girl who won your heart becomes salty, sour, or even bitter; she may lose some of her former physical attractiveness. (The man may do this, too, of course!) More fundamentally, each one reveals the essence of fallen humanity. Not long after the honeymoon (if not before), pride, selfishness, stubbornness, laziness, impatience, and other flaws rear their ugly heads. Even worse, at our best we are seldom able to listen well enough, understand fully, or give completely of ourselves. Soon, our high expectations crash upon the rocks of reality. The one whom we idolized now becomes someone whom we find difficult to respect. We struggle with disappointment, which expresses itself in nagging and criticism, or simply neglect.

What has happened? We have forgotten that our spouse is created in the image of God. Focusing on his or her faults, which are evidence of our common fall from God's glory, we overlook the essential beauty and worth of God's image-bearer. In other words, we swing from one extreme to another: from imagining that our spouse is divine to forgetting that he or she is human, and possesses fundamental dignity. Rather than looking for, and appreciating, the vestiges of God's excellence in our mate, we focus on the symptoms of his or her sinfulness. Instead of being thankful for the other's virtues and God-implanted abilities, we concentrate upon his or her flaws and failings. No relationship can flourish in a climate of mutual disrespect, and marriage is no exception. By withholding appreciation, we sow seeds of sadness and then sullen resentment, as each one feels unjustly rejected.

Neglecting God's Revelation

Adam and Eve knew God. They heard him speak in the

---

93 2 Cor 4:18; 5:7.

garden and saw his wonderful works all around them. Unique to all other created beings, the man and the woman were recipients of God's revelation and were meant to continue in close fellowship with their Creator by listening to his word and responding to him in faith. If any married couple desires to fulfill God's purpose for their life together, they must also orient their lives around his revelation, especially the written words of the Bible. Instead, most people today fill their ears, eyes, and minds with other words and other voices, which drown out the only Word that can bring life and happiness.

Only a few generations ago, it was common for American families to gather around the hearth in the evenings and on Sunday afternoons to listen to the head of the household read from the big family Bible. Most families attended church regularly and prayed together around the table. They knew many passages of the Scriptures by heart, they could sing hymns from memory, and public oratory and popular literature were replete with references from God's Word. Much of this has changed today. Church attendance has declined precipitously, as shopping malls and amusement parks are thronged with crowds of consumers and fun-seekers. The television blares away in nearly every room, unless the radio is on. Everywhere you go, you see people listening to music or something else on a portable device of some sort, texting or talking into their cell phones, glued to the computer screen, reading something on the Internet or watching the latest performance on YouTube.

At school, children are taught that the Bible is full of errors, or never hear of God at all. Many church sermons, when heard, consist of uplifting stories of people who derived some practical benefit, such as good health or material wealth, from believing in a God who bears hardly any resemblance to the God of Abraham, Moses, Jesus, and Paul. Even among evangelical Christians, very few read their Bibles daily, and those who do rarely follow a plan or engage in serious study of the Scriptures.[94] How many Christians

---

94 A recent LifeWay Research study found only 45 percent of those who regularly attend church read the Bible more than once a week. Over 40

make a regular practice of memorizing passages from the Bible? How many couples read the Bible together?

The absence of God's revelation, coupled with the pounding presence of a cacophony of other voices, produces confusion at best, and seriously disordered lives at worst. Rather than making decisions based on the commands of Christ, couples argue over whose desires should be dominant. When they are faced with a crisis, most people turn to their own resources first, instead of searching the Scriptures to seek God's mind, or claiming his promises to calm their fears.

Conflicts naturally arise in marriage, and could be solved in biblical ways, but most couples today just fight it out, or withdraw into a stony silence, leaving themselves vulnerable to temptations to foster intimacy with someone else. If husbands knew the love of Christ, they would be able to forgive and love their wives; if wives trusted in the love of God the Father, they would be able to submit to their imperfect mates. If either knew the plan of God, they would try to avoid the ways of the world and build a relationship based upon God's revealed will.

Instead, we squander valuable time on frivolous entertainment; our conversations differ little, if at all, from what is said by unbelievers in their homes; children fail to receive instruction in godliness; and the entire family is left without a spiritual compass. There is no anchor to keep them from being tossed to and fro by fads, no spring of living water to bring refreshment and joy, no word of truth to protect them from falsehood.

How do you turn to God in effectual prayer if you do not know who he is or what to pray for? If you are not daily being informed, even reformed, by his words, how can you mature into a loving person? Forgiveness of others is almost impossible unless we receive God's promise of mercy in our own regular times of Bible reading, meditation,and prayer. Failure to feed on God's

---

percent of the people attending read their Bible occasionally, maybe once or twice a month. Almost 1 in 5 churchgoers say they never read the Bible—essentially the same number who read it every day. See http://www.christianitytoday.com/edstetzer/2015/july/epidemic-of-bible-illiteracy-in-our-churches.html

revelation in the Bible deprives a couple of the only foundation for a stable marriage, one built upon faith in God's truth, love for each other stemming from a keen sense of his love for us, and hearts brimming with hope.

Male-Female Conflict

As we have seen, men and women, though fundamentally the same as human beings created in the image of God, reflect that image in distinct ways. We have different characteristics and desires, or at least similar ones held with markedly disproportionate intensity. Although these differences are meant by God to be beneficial to our marriages, they can often cause great confusion and pain.

Living in a fallen world, we face daily stress, perhaps more than ever before in history. Men and women react differently to stress. Women tend respond to prolonged stress with depression, phobias, hysterias, and anorexia much more than men, who react to chronic stress by becoming more aggressive and having higher levels of energy, which can lead to a greater frequency of cardiovascular illness, as well as an increased susceptibility to infectious diseases. Men and women are stressed by different aspects of their environment, too. If women are not happy in their social sphere, especially the nuclear family, they become depressed, whereas men feel more stress when they are frustrated in achieving their goals or sense a loss of control over their surroundings. Lack of sexual fulfillment or respect from their wife and family also produce high stress for men.

At such times, good communication is essential if the marriage bond is to be strengthened, but communication difficulties plague the man-and-wife relationship, partly because of our innate gender differences. When a woman does not feel free to talk with her husband, expressing her joys and sorrows at length in a safe environment, she feels estranged from him. Seeking to build the relationship by revealing her heart, she feels abandoned if he fails to spend time with her, if he belittles her feelings, especially her fears, or if he seeks to solve her problem instead of just listening. Men often don't realize that if they will simply allow their wife to talk until she thinks he has really heard her, she will feel much better and the original cause of her unhappiness may seem less important to her. It will still eventually be necessary to address the problem, of course, so the husband shouldn't just forget about it or consider it trivial. What we are talking about now is the importance of listening with loving attention.

Both because of their role as leaders in the home, and because of their pride as fallen human beings, men want respect from their wives. I can't say this often or strongly enough! If his wife fails to show respect, a man will respond with anger and perhaps withdrawal into himself, his hobbies, recreation, work, Internet pornography, or even another woman. Thus, when a man expresses his frustration about work or sex, his wife should patiently listen, rather than offering advice or criticism. Strangely enough, both the advice and the criticism will come across to him as disrespect! Women may wonder at this, since they freely offer advice to each other in times of trouble. As we saw earlier, however, men tend to want to figure things out by themselves first, before consulting an "expert" for his opinion. Notice I said "his" opinion. Men will listen to those whom they have asked for guidance, who are usually other men, but find a woman's unsolicited suggestions to be affronts to their manhood, particularly if the words come from the mouth of their wife.

This sort of resistance to a wife's well-meant advice may reflect sinful pride, of course. The book of Proverbs repeatedly urges its readers, who are mostly addressed as males, to accept counsel and even rebuke.[95] The sad fact is, however, that in this fallen world (remember, we are in the chapter on "The Bad"), men do not want to hear much correction, criticism, or counsel from their wives. Only after forty-seven years of being married to Dori did I admit that I had been foolish in being so unwilling to listen to her advice so much of the time.

"Yes! It's been really frustrating to me!" she responded.

I went on, "Most of what you say has been right. The problem is that there is so much of it!"

---

95   See, for example, Prov 1 25, 30; 8:14; 12:15; 13:10; 19:20; 27:9 (on counsel); on receiving rebuke, Prov 13:1;17:10; 27:5).

Dori and I are not unique. Most men I've talked with agree that they bristle when their wives offer unsolicited reminders, critiques, advice, instruction, or admonitions.

Of course, if we were more secure in the love of God for us in Christ; more aware of our shortcomings, including our ignorance; more appreciative of our wife's good sense; more eager to learn; and especially more assured of our wife's respect for us–then we might be more open to unasked advice.

When we rush in with what we consider to be our wise counsel or well-deserved rebukes, we may also be revealing our pride, self-confidence, and a certain disdain for the other person. If we could only see God's image in our spouse, we would stand in awe and sit in reverent reticence until the time came for courteous, caring speech.

During courtship, a woman will do all sorts of things just to be with her man. She will accompany him in his recreation gladly, giving him the impression that she actually enjoys the activities. After marriage, he may find that she really wasn't interested in what they were doing, only in being close to him. But he very much wants a recreational companion, a playmate, so he feels let down.

A wife wants to be sure that her husband is faithful to her, so she looks for open, honest communication of what he is doing, especially how he is spending his time away from her. By hiding this from her, he may evoke in her an anxiety that he is seeing another woman.

Although a man may be attracted to a woman's appearance before marriage, after the honeymoon, many wives let themselves go physically. Perhaps they cut their hair shorter than their husband would like, gain weight, and fail to dress in a feminine way at home. Then they wonder why his former ardor seems to have cooled!

When Paul says, "Let the wife *see* that she respects *her* husband,"[96] he is speaking to a profound desire men have to be admired by their wives. Sure, they also seek the affirmation of their colleagues at work, but if a man's wife does not show respect,

---

96 Eph 5:33.

he feels like a failure. The difficulty is that most women have no clue about this deep longing that men have, or how to fulfill it. They may express lack of respect unwittingly, by asking questions that seem innocent enough ("Did you remember to lock the door?") but which communicate lack of trust and confidence in his abilities.[97] Husbands also feel looked down upon, even treated like little boys, when their wives constantly nag them or scold them. That's not to say that they don't deserve it; often they do. But a self-righteous, critical tone of voice may evoke sullen resentment or even an angry outburst.

Perhaps to put this in perspective, we might ask, How would a wife feel if her husband frequently pointed out her mistakes; commented negatively on her appearance, her cooking, her treatment of the children, or her housework; or otherwise indicated that he disapproved of her?

That reminds us that when their husbands do not speak words of affection and affirmation to them, wives tend to feel rejected, even if they aren't. No one really likes to be put down! All of us appreciate appropriate words of praise, thanks, and love. Husbands, though they don't like what they think are "negative" words, do not realize how much their wives crave positive words. If they don't hear appreciative comments about their character, their good ideas, their hard work, their appearance, their cooking and housework, their care for the children, their kindness to others, wives tend to lose heart. And who can blame them?

When a wife feels unloved, she may complain, criticize, or even lash out in anger. The husband takes this as an attack, and either fights back or, more often, withdraws. This drives his wife crazy, because—and this is the part men find almost incomprehensible—her negative words are really an attempt to draw close to him. Remember that women communicate to build relationships, while men communicate to transact business. So, wives hope that their words of dissatisfaction or anger will evoke

---

97 There are times for such questions, of course. If a man is chronically irresponsible or forgetful of vital tasks, his wife should find a way to alert him to this and ask him how and when she may remind him.

a response of listening, caring, and comforting. Far from intending to drive her husband away, the wife is really hoping to create a stronger bond between them, by letting him know what is on her heart so that he can come beside her as her companion and encourager.

The husband does not see it that way, of course. In male language, criticism equals attack, and is met with a counter-attack or a strategic retreat, depending on how strong he thinks he is relative to the attacker. But his wife sees withdrawal as abandonment, the very thing she fears the most. When he clams up or walks away, she thinks he has rejected her. The intimacy she had hoped to foster has eluded her and turned into a deeper sense of distance.

Women are often quick to say, "If my husband wants respect, he needs to earn it." From one standpoint, that's fair enough, and a man should do all that he can to act in such a way that his wife can be proud of him and look up to him. We will discuss this more later, but for now we should just be clear that women must keep a diligent watch on their attitudes and speech if they are to communicate admiration and confidence towards their husbands. Even if a woman finds it hard to respect her husband in her heart, she can at least treat him with respect and courtesy, just as she would anyone else in authority. If she doesn't, she will find a growing distance developing between herself and her husband and will even risk his being tempted to find a woman who does make him (temporarily) feel good about himself.

Loving Leadership?

We have seen that God's original blueprint for marriage calls for the husband to serve his wife as a loving leader, and for her to submit to him as a suitable helper. Ever since the Fall, however, this natural order of things has been disrupted, with the consequent "battle of the sexes" and its attendant miseries. Where was Adam when the serpent tempted Eve? He had received clear revelation from God and should have been on hand to help his wife resist the wiles of the evil one. He had deserted his post as moral and spiritual captain of that couple, with disastrous results for all subsequent generations. Not long after Adam and Eve disobeyed God, God spoke to the woman and said, "Your desire *shall be* for your husband, and he shall rule over you."[98] In recent years, I think, the correct interpretation of this aspect of the curse upon fallen mankind has come to light. Just as sin desired to control Cain,[99] so the woman desires to rule over her husband. Men, however, want to be in control, and since they are usually bigger and stronger, they tend to "rule over" their wives. In modern society, we have seen a retreat from this usual situation to some degree, so that the wife often dominates her husband.

In general, however, men "rule the roost," for good or ill. All too often, their authority is used for selfish ends, bringing untold sorrow upon their wives and children. A man can depart from God's original design in two basic ways: dereliction of duty and domineering dominion. A woman can only follow or submit if her husband exercises leadership. But if he withdraws, most women will tend to move into that power vacuum out of what they consider to be necessity. His refusal to make decisions forces her to make the final choice. His avoidance of responsibility tempts her to assume the burden. The sad fact is that men often seem to be as irresponsible as Adam when he blamed his disobedience upon his wife,[100] and women seem to be as prone as was their primal mother to take the lead.

Husbands desert their posts when they fail to listen, neglect to partner with and lead their wives in planning, put off making decisions, cave in to follow anything their wives want, or bury themselves in work or entertainment. When a man doesn't exercise the initiative to find out what his wife desires or fears, and take steps to accommodate her legitimate longings, he forfeits respect. By failing to initiate family Bible reading and prayer, or educating the children in the ways of God, a Christian husband loses credibility as a spiritual leader. Lack of leadership can take

---

98 Gen 3:16.
99 Gen 4:7.
100 Gen 3:12.

other forms as well, such as lying in bed while his wife gets up to go out to work in the morning, perhaps to a job she doesn't like but is just doing to help him with the finances. I did this for the first few months of marriage, until I learned how alone my wife felt when she had to get herself off with no help or encouragement from me. Even in today's world, where most wives work outside the home, they want a husband who takes responsibility for providing financial security. In fact, many wives resent having to leave home to go to work, especially after they have children.

Men are also called to lead by investing time in their children. If the husband neglects his family and spends all his free time watching the television, playing video games, reading, working in the yard or the shop, or having fun with his male friends, his wife and children will feel abandoned. Even when he says he must put in extra hours at work, though she may at first consider this a valid excuse, after a while she begins to resent his work and his absence from family life. She knows, after all, that children need a father, and not for just a minute or two each day, which is all that many men expend on their children.

On the other hand, some men do take the reins in their homes, but in a proud and domineering fashion. The man who always insists that he is right, who does not seek his wife's advice before making a decision and brooks no questions or comments, or who reacts angrily when he is crossed—such a man is only a dictator, not a leader. He's a petty tyrant who wants his way no matter what and reacts like a two-year-old when his orders are not immediately obeyed or his pleasures instantly gratified. Imagine how much resentment his wife and children are storing up as each day passes. Things only get worse if he resorts to shouting or even physical violence to maintain control. Once a blow has been inflicted on her body by the one who was supposed to nourish, cherish, and protect her, a woman takes a long time to recover any trust in her husband, or affection towards him.

A Suitable Helper?

Lest we think that only men contribute to the battle of the

sexes, we need to remember that Yahweh said, "Your desire *shall be* for your husband."[101] That is, as I said earlier, the woman will want to gain control over the man, rule him, and generally usurp his God-given authority. Perhaps Eve had wandered away from Adam as he tilled the garden, removing herself from his protection. What was she doing near the forbidden tree, anyway? Why did she even enter into a conversation with the snake? How much better it would have been if she had stayed by her husband or run back to him quickly! Independence can be a good trait, but it can turn into rebellion when a wife seeks to go her own way and depart from her husband's care and supervision.

We can understand why wives would want to be recognized for who they are and given scope for their talents and interests to be developed, and how a husband's refusal to honor his wife could evoke an urge towards autonomy. At the same time, we can also see how disobedience and insubordination are deeply rooted in all of our hearts. A woman who frequently questions her husband's judgment, counters his wishes, critiques his actions, and contradicts his commands to the children will reap a very bitter harvest of resentment and perhaps worse. Constant nagging communicates profound disrespect. More subtle is the tendency in many, perhaps most, women, to want to reform their husbands. The intention to make him over may be present long before the wedding, but it shows up in suggestions, complaints, and even ultimatums afterwards. If he is treated like a little boy in this way, he may respond with puerile resistance, like a sullen, stubborn teenager. Other reactions include withdrawal into work or play or, all too frequently, finding a woman who makes him "feel like a man" – temporarily, at least.

One of the tragedies of our time is that our culture dismisses, and even denies, the honorable role of a woman as helper to her husband and mother to her children. Rather than being encouraged to concentrate their energies upon home and family, women are expected to spend the most productive hours of their day outside of the home, building a career or at least making money. Some

---

101 Gen 3:16.

of this emphasis, of course, reflects the creation of woman in the image of God and her capacity to contribute to society and to the economy. That, indeed, is the focus of Proverbs 31

Much more often, economic necessity seems to dictate that a wife work outside the home to provide necessary income.

In its current form, however, this recognition of the enormous range of abilities that God has bestowed on women has been twisted in a direction almost new to human history, and not necessarily better. If a woman's worth derives from her performance outside the home, then husbands and children are all too often left to fend for themselves, with truly awful psychological and social consequences, not to mention the negative effects of these expectations on women themselves.

Though some husbands deeply appreciate the value of a wife who pours most of her strength and thought into loving him and their children, as the Bible teaches,[102] too many do not see just how much they need such a helper at home. They either fail to express gratitude and sincere admiration for the domestic accomplishments of their wife, or even belittle her efforts. Such attitudes can crush a woman's spirit and drive her out the door to find affirmation in the workplace.[103] Not having been taught the value of a stay-at-home wife and mother, women often only think of their worth in terms of the prestige or salary of a career or paying job. Most, indeed, still consider family and home to be highly important, and seek to balance their lives by strenuous effort, but the attempt often fails. Doing well at work leaves little time for thought about home, and hours spent on the job consume energy that could otherwise be put into loving husband and children.[104]

As I noted above, financial pressures often seem to require

---

102 See, for example, Tit 2:4–5; 1 Tim 5:10, 14,

103 For more on the worth of a godly wife, see G. Wright Doyle, *More Precious than Rubies*, http://www.reachingchineseworldwide.org/more-precious-than-rubies. PDF e-book.

104 For a very balanced perspective on "balancing," see https://www.ucg.org/the-good-news/career-home-and-family-can-women-really-do-it-all

the wife to bring in a second income. Truly, for some couples the husband's paycheck does not suffice, but for many couples the question is not how much he makes, but how much they want to spend. Rising expectations have thrust us into a standard of living unprecedented in human history, one which far exceeds our real needs. Maybe financial crises and recessions can reset the standards, but we have gone so far that it will be hard to turn back to the days when a simple house and a usable car would do. College education has become prohibitively expensive, so many young couples enter marriage with enormous student debt, or they are trying to save for their children's future tuition payments. However, there are ways to get a university degree without working like a slave for twenty years or taking out student loans.[105]

While most wives work outside the home, most men still expect their wives to cook, keep the house clean and neat, and take primary care of the children. Men often resent helping with housework, as it takes time away from more enjoyable activities that they would like to pursue after work hours. But a woman who works full-time outside the home just like her husband will of course come back equally exhausted. She is often too tired to prepare dinner or listen to her children talk about their day, much less to her husband's stories of success and failure at his job. If he does not do what she considers to be his fair share of the housework and childcare, then she feels cheated, and if she does not meet his expectations for a companion, housekeeper, and mother, then he is likewise unhappy.

Couples either need to learn to live on the man's income alone, or adjustments must be made. In my opinion, if a man insists upon having his wife take a full-time job, or if financial needs make it necessary that she work outside the home, then he must commit to helping her with half of her domestic duties. On the other hand, if her job is more a result of her own ambition and drive, then she must bite the bullet and find time to care for their home and children, without neglecting her husband, which many

---

105 Many universities and colleges now allow students to earn a degree by taking courses online. There are also many ways of acquiring a marketable skill that does not require a college education.

women find almost impossible. It is no wonder that marital stress has increased in recent decades.[106]

Failure to Leave Parents

A great deal of marital trouble stems from a failure to leave one's parents. Not only do we have to leave our parents physically, but we must depart emotionally. This failure to leave can be seen both in our own sinfulness, which is sometimes learned from our parents, as well as in the way we react to our spouse's sinfulness, which may remind us of our parents.

If a man brings his wife into his parents' home, she will almost inevitably come into conflict with his mother. He will be forced to choose between them, and sorrow and sadness will result. If he puts his mother first, his wife will feel rejected and begin to nurse resentment. As a consequence, the wife may build an abnormally close relationship with her children, especially her sons, who may come to displace their father in her affections, causing untold misery. On the other hand, if the husband tries to protect his wife and demonstrates that the wife is now first in his life, his mother may feel abandoned, particularly if her own relationship with her husband is not very close. She may take out her frustration upon her daughter-in-law, making things even more difficult for her son and his bride. A man living with either his own or his wife's parents can be equally problematic as the husband is unable to establish his headship of his own family.

Today, however, most young couples live separately from their parents. Despite this physical distance, unhealthy emotional ties may continue to bind children to their fathers and mothers in such a way that their marriages suffer. For example, most of us carry mental and emotional baggage from our childhood, especially from ways in which our parents failed to show us perfect love. After all, even the best parents are both finite and fallen, and cannot provide the sort of love balanced with truth that children need. More than that, however, despite their good

---

106 For practical advice on how to escape from this trap, see Larry Burkett's *Women Leaving the Workplace*.

intentions, parents grievously hurt their children, and leave them with wounds that can fester for decades.

For a very long time, which are also the most formative years, our parents are the most important people in our life, and their words carry incredible power, lodging in our minds and binding us to wrong thoughts that can cripple us emotionally. "Curses" – that is, statements that sometimes have the effect of seeming to bind us to a negative destiny - that they have uttered may define our self-image and keep us from being all that God intends us to become. "You're a sissy!" "You are stupid!" "You just can't do anything right!" "We didn't really want to have you, you know." Because we are made in the image of God, as children we reacted with outrage at our parents' sins, and rightly so. But our own sinful nature immediately enters into the picture, and our righteous indignation quickly becomes resentment, self-pity, disrespect, fear, and other negative thought patterns. Children often make what John and Paula Sandford have called "inner vows" in reaction to painful experiences in early years.[107]

Often, these disappointments lie hidden beneath the surface of our conscious thoughts, exercising their baneful influence from behind the scenes. It is uncanny how we often marry someone who "happens" to lack the same good qualities that our parents lacked or have the same faults that most irritated us in our father or mother. The result is that the slightest action or attitude that resembles some failing of one's parents will evoke powerful emotions, such as rage, fear, or disgust. When this happens, we are reacting not just to our spouse, but to years of anger, terror, or revulsion that we felt towards our parents and from which we have not yet been delivered.

In other words, we are still in bondage to our childhood, and have not yet "left" father and mother. A little boy who was nagged and criticized by his mother will probably respond with disproportionate rage when his wife offers even the slightest

---

107 See & Paula Sandford, *The Transformation of the Inner Man.*, 191-206. Though I do not agree with everything in this book, I consider it to be one of the most helpful I have every read, and strongly recommend it.

criticism or suggestion. If a father does not affirm his daughter's femininity by showing affection for her, noticing her, and telling her that she is pretty, she may grow up with an excessive longing for a man's attention, affection, and approval, and may make demands on her husband that no man can meet. Was your father addicted to alcohol? Don't be surprised if you either marry an alcoholic or become one yourself. If the connection with your past is not so obvious—perhaps you and your spouse are both temperate—then there may be a less obvious resemblance, such as a tendency to become dependent upon food or some other comfort, or a great fear of a certain type of behavior that your father manifested when he had drunk too much.

All too often, we also fail to leave behind habits, value systems, and assumptions that our parents passed down to us that conflict with the biblical perspective. Perhaps we have an obsession with some goal that our parents held to be necessary for a happy life, such as acquisition of money, power, and status. A father may have stressed athletic prowess; a mother may have inculcated a conviction that beauty is essential for personal value. They may have cherished hatred against relatives, the government, or people of another religion or race. Perhaps they had unhelpful or unloving ways of communicating, or had an inordinate love of comfort, popularity, pleasure, or entertainment. If these were held too closely, and mattered too much, they were false gods, unable to give life and leading only to death. All these false values can interfere with marital harmony by putting us into conflict with each other or by demanding so much time and energy that they pull us away from focusing on one another.

Failure to Be Fruitful and Take Dominion

We have already seen that having children is a normal part of marriage. Not infrequently, when couples try to avoid childbirth by birth control or abortion, they are standing in opposition to God's original design. We show lack of trust in God when we allow fear to keep us from bring children into the world. We also consign ourselves to a self-centered life, one which grows narrower and narrower as the years pass. It is often too late before couples realize that their window of opportunity has closed, and that they will never have the joy of caring for little people who reflect their love for each other; of helping children grow into mature, loving people who trust and serve God; of holding a grandchild in one's arms. And who will take care of them when they grow old and feeble?

We often fail to steward even our own bodies. It might surprise you, but a large proportion of marital tension these days results from poor health. Sometimes, instead of nourishing our bodies, we seek instant gratification through excessive consumption of junk food. Rather than exercising, we sit lazily in front of the television. Instead of making adequate time for rest, we wear ourselves out surfing the Internet late at night or over-committing ourselves, even to serving God or the church. We even become addicted to harmful substances. Or perhaps we simply don't make health a priority. Someone who is in bad physical condition will be challenged to carry out all the tasks necessary for successful homemaking or providing financially for the family, however, and will make a poor sexual companion. If you are tired, your patience wears thin more quickly, and you are certainly not much in the mood for lovemaking. Headaches and stomach aches will distract you from caring for others and concentrate your attention on yourself. Obesity has become a national epidemic that not only leads to a variety of illnesses, but can kill one's self-respect, attractiveness, and libido. Respect forms an essential component of marital happiness, but it's hard to admire someone who, because of failure to stay fit, is flabby or listless. Bad habits add up over the years, causing serious conditions, and can lead to an early, expensive, and painful death.[108]

Eros Defiled

"And be joined [cleave, cling] to his wife, and they shall become one flesh."[109]

---

108 For more information on physical, mental, and spiritual health, see my book, *The Lord's Healing Words*.
109 Gen 2:24.

Several decades ago, a book by John White[110] told of how romantic love (*eros*) has become defiled by sexual sin. Things have only gotten worse since then. What God intended to be a beautiful, bonding fusion of man and wife has been corrupted almost beyond recognition.

Surveys indicate that most people nowadays enter marriage with sexual experience. What a tragedy! You cannot count on the purity of your bride or groom. Lurking in the background is the knowledge (or the memory) of a previous intimate relationship. How will marriage compare with pre-marital indulgence? Will my spouse love me as passionately as my lover did? Will I "perform" as well as that other partner did? Sexually-transmitted diseases don't simply disappear when the wedding ring is slipped upon your finger. They linger on, as constant reminders of a selfish loss of control, and ongoing threats to health and happiness.

Accompanying all this folly and sin is a load of guilt and shame that hinders sexual intimacy. What was meant to be beautiful beyond description has assumed an ugly face that mocks our longing for what could have been, and what should be. With divorce at epidemic levels, models of patient endurance and forbearance are lacking for newly-married couples. No wonder that so many decide to call it quits within the first few years! They have only their parents' example to guide them, so they perpetuate the cycle of falling in and out of love, making and breaking promises, and increasing hardness of heart. Has any generation begun married life with so much emotiional baggage, and so many resources for making the physical relationship that God created to express his own beauty and love turned into such a source of ugliness and lust?

Within marriage itself, men tend to use sex to satisfy their desires rather than to express love, and women withhold their bodies to express dissatisfaction. If a woman does not receive non-sexual expressions of affection almost daily, she becomes less inclined to want to have physical relations. Her husband, on the other hand, sees "affection" mostly as sex, and tends to rush towards

---

110 John White, *Eros Defiled*. Downers Grove, IL: Inter-Varsity Press, 1977.

an erotic encounter before engaging in those things that his wife sees as necessary affection and foreplay. Although sometimes a wife's excuses are legitimate, perhaps subconsciously, she may sometimes try to find reasons to put off her husband's advances and delay sexual relations. "I'm tired." "I have a headache." "My back hurts." "Not now." With these words, she pours cold water on her mate's ardor, sowing a field of frustration that can reap very bitter consequences.

With the whole modern world engulfed in a mad rush for money, status, power, and pleasure, countless couples wear themselves out, leaving little time or energy for intimacy of any kind. All too often, men busy themselves with their work or their hobbies, while women—often exhausted from work outside the home—try to clean up the house or spend precious time with the children. Indeed, a mother's normal care for her offspring can distract her from the very real sexual needs of her husband, who quite frequently feels displaced. Investing hopes and dreams in work can also lead to emotional involvement with the people at work, which saps the vitality of a husband or wife's love for their spouse. Churches and other service organizations are not free from this form of temptation, as people are joined in a common cause that energizes them and gives great joy in doing something good for others. What begins as unity of purpose can all too easily spiral into a closer union of minds, hearts, and finally, bodies.

As if all this were not bad enough, the Internet and readily-available DVDs have ensnared countless men, making them slaves of pornography and sexual fantasies. These offer excitement and temporary relief from tension but render normal sexual intimacy with their wife less and less possible. If a wife discovers that her husband is addicted in this way, she feels betrayed and abandoned, though she might not realize her possible role in her spouse's obsession. Although pornography is increasingly used by women, they are usually more affected by romance novels or romantic movies where the men are always handsome, charming, and passionate. They grow more and more dissatisfied with their boring, distant, and perhaps disgusting husbands. What happened to the fit man who caught her fancy, who spoke sweet words and brought chocolate and flowers? Why doesn't he suggest a date at the movie or a quiet restaurant, or an exciting outing anymore?

Cleaving to Another

Frustrated in marriage, countless people "fall in love" with someone else. "Sudden" romances usually aren't as "out of the blue" as they appear to be. Usually, we are already vulnerable, because of disappointment with our current spouse, and we are perhaps more than a little bit on the lookout for someone better. Men who have been feeding their discontent by watching pornographic material on the Internet or indulging greedy gazes at attractive women, especially since fashion dictates the display of more skin than it once did, will be harboring ticking time bombs in their hearts.

For husbands, a prettier woman may come along with a softer smile and a more appreciative attitude towards you than your critical, contrary, and complaining wife. Or you may be attracted to someone who looks the way your wife did when you were pursuing her. Likewise, for wives, there may be a more kind, considerate, thoughtful, attractive man who really seems to care about you. He listens when you tell him how difficult things are for you and offers to help with little things. He seems so patient, so understanding, so unlike your husband, who is too busy with work or computer games to spend time with you or the kids.

It doesn't take much of a spark to ignite a flame that can consume your mind and emotions within a matter of weeks or even days. Thinking of your new love constantly, you can't wait for the next time to talk or see each other. You hate to have to say, "Goodbye," or, worse, "Good night." You have finally found the person for whom you have always been looking. Alas, your decision to marry your current spouse seems like an awful mistake. You decide that you missed God's choice for you! All his or her faults now seem magnified in comparison with your new friend.

Longings you never knew you had well up within you and find expression in words, gestures, and perhaps more. Soon, you are allowing intimacies you would have never considered possible. Your judgment has been overwhelmed by passion, and it doesn't seem to matter. You feel so good with the other person that you forget, or choose to ignore, the warning signals that tell you of danger ahead. Heedless, you plunge forward into what can only lead to disaster—for your marriage, your children, the other person, and yourself.

We don't need to have "been there" and "done that" to know how this sad story usually ends, with misery for everyone involved. Reading any of the countless novels, plays, and stories, from *Lancelot and Guinevere* to *Anna Karenina* to *Dr. Zhivago*, will tell us the basic plot, which is almost always a tragedy. So how do we either avoid or overcome such an onslaught of feelings, emotions that can destroy all that we once held dear? How do we keep from being just another character in an old, old story? Several biblical principles, which we shall look at later, can help guide our way.

The Downward Spiral

As differences and distractions breed distrust, disdain, and perhaps even disgust, couples plunge into a downward spiral that can become a vortex of relational death. Conflicts go unresolved. Slights and offences fester in sad and sullen hearts. Grudges grow into high walls of hatred. The tokens of affection that once brought pleasure somehow don't come as often as before, and two people who once adored each other become merely housemates rather than true companions.

If this corrosive process is not halted soon enough, the couple may end up living separately, making way for divorce. Or, they can settle down for a long winter of discontent, dully doing their duty. Although doing our duty is a valid motive to stay married, in itself, it doesn't heal the gaping wound in our hearts, nor does it enable us to face the day with cheerfulness and hope. We may have avoided the terrible (and irreparable) damage that divorce inflicts on everyone involved, but we have not equipped ourselves to rebuild the marriage. We are stuck in survival mode, nothing more.

Adultery, alienation, separation, and divorce turn marriage from a picture of the relationship between God and his people into a tragic parody of what was meant to be. Instead of faithfulness and unconditional love, there is infidelity and rejection. Rather than tender, loving leadership, we see neglect or abuse by the man, and insolent resistance by the woman. "Till death parts us" and "as long as we both shall live" may have been spoken sincerely at the wedding ceremony, but times have changed. We decide we don't want to take this anymore; we have a "right" to be happy; indeed, (we say to ourselves, and often with our friends' agreement) God wants us to be happy, and not live in this hell of a relationship. Forget Yahweh remaining faithful to faithless Israel, or Christ nourishing and cherishing his very unlovely bride. I'm out of here! No wonder non-Christians look at the high divorce rate among churchgoers and wonder whether faith in Christ makes any difference when push comes to shove. But it doesn't have to be this bad, or end in ugliness! Marriage can be a beautiful experience—not perfect, of course, but lovely in its own way.

CHAPTER THREE

THE BEAUTIFUL:
A DEEPER PURPOSE
FOR MARRIAGE

We have seen that God established marriage for our good, and that it brings many pleasures and benefits, such as companionship, collaboration in fruitful labor, the enjoyment of marital sexual relations and the children that follow, and much more. In our fallen world, however, many forces combine to hinder us from realizing the potential of this God-ordained relationship.

The Bible teaches, and our daily experience confirms, that we are all afflicted with a debilitating disease called sin. Unless God halts the progress of it, this illness is also degenerative, and will lead to temporal and eternal death. But, for believers, God has intervened, and has begun to reverse the process of our descent into hell on earth and in eternity. Part of that great reversal is the remarkable change he effects in us by the Holy Spirit as we trust in him, a change so profound that Paul calls that changed part of us our "new man."[111] With God's energy empowering us, and his truth enlightening us, we don't have to live as we used to, in darkness and depravity; now we can begin to imitate the character of Christ, growing daily in our likeness to him. Following this path, God provides both a certain degree of happiness in marriage and

---

111 Eph 4:24; Col 3:10.

the possibility that the marriage itself will gradually grow into something beautiful.

If we are to overcome the resistance we find inside ourselves, we must first understand one major purpose that God has for marriage: our growth in holiness. "He chose us in him before the foundation of the world, that we should be holy and without blame before him."[112] The theme of this verse resounds throughout the Bible: "You shall be holy; for I *am* holy."[113] Christ died for the church in order that he might sanctify her.[114] God's eternal plan calls for us to be conformed to the moral image of his Son Jesus.[115] Without holiness, we cannot ever see God.[116] Thus, when Paul affirms that God is working all things together for the good of those who love him, he means, primarily, our *spiritual* good.

Everything that God allows to happen is designed to make us more like Christ.[117] So, if we are to reap the full benefit of marriage, we must make friends with God's plan for our life, which is to fashion us more and more into the moral likeness of Jesus.[118] We will not be able to handle the daily disappointments that come, much less the huge ones that will inevitably arise when two sinners live together, if we do not see them as part of God's program for us; indeed, we must see them as an integral and essential aspect of his will for us in this life.

In addition to God's plan for sanctifying us, we must also reorient our minds to face marriage with an entirely new goal: to give, rather than to receive. "Love your neighbor as you love yourself."[119] "It is more blessed to give than to receive."[120] These simple but profound truths can set us free from bondage to our

---

112 Eph 1:4.
113 Lev 11:44–45; 1 Pet 1:16.
114 Eph 5:26.
115 1 John 3:2.
116 Heb 12:14.
117 Rom 8:28.
118 Eph 4:24.
119 Mat 19:19.
120 Acts 20:35.

spouse's limited ability to love us, or even their dislike of us, now that our flaws have also become painfully evident to them. Instead of pinning my happiness on how another treats me, I can focus on treating him or her with unselfish love, seeking nothing other than the satisfaction of obeying God, imitating Christ, and blessing the person who once won my heart and evoked a promise of lifelong commitment from me.

In other words, we are to place our hope in God, not in our spouse. At the right time and in the right way, he will recompense us for faith and obedience. We may have to wait until we die or until Jesus returns, but our efforts are never in vain. "Whatever good anyone does, he will receive the same from the Lord."[121] Of course, we don't obey in order to earn salvation or gain earthly benefits, but to show our gratitude for God's grace and receive his commendation.

As Emerson Eggerichs writes, "I have concluded that we don't have a 'marriage crisis' in the Christian community; we have a crisis of faith."[122] "A man's unconditional love for his wife reveals his love for Christ ... A wife's unconditional respect for her husband reveals her reverence for Christ ... In the ultimate sense, your marriage has nothing to do with your spouse. It has everything to do with your relationship to Jesus Christ."[123] We shall fail, of course. When we do, we can repent, confess, get up, and try again. "Ultimately, you practice love or respect because beyond your spouse you see Jesus Christ and you envision a moment when you will be standing before him at the final judgment, realizing that your marriage was really a tool and a test to deepen and demonstrate your love and your reverence for your Lord."[124] Christians have the truth of God and the Spirit of Christ within them, so they are free to respond with love rather than with the hate that comes so naturally to us. We can be spiritually and internally free under any

---

121 Eph 6:7–8.
122 Eggerichs, *Love and Respect,* 276.
123 Eggerichs, *Love and Respect,* 279.
124 Eggerichs, *Love and Respect,* 279-80.

circumstances; we are not bound by our spouse's limitations in love or respect.[125]

As we live out our faith, hope, and love towards God, we leave a precious legacy, for our children are watching. They will take note and imitate either our disobedience or our efforts to follow Christ. Even if they have already grown up, a change in their parents' marriage will bring them new hope and perhaps even change them as adults. If both partners are seeking to please God in their marriage, they can create a team that combines all that is good in each of them, shining God's light into a dark world.

Love This Man, This Woman

Many wedding ceremonies include a question like this: "Do you take this woman to be your wife? ... Do you take this man to be your husband?" I did not realize the significance of that little word "this" until just recently. When we answer this question, "I do," we are pledging to love the person standing next to us, not the person we hope he or she will be once desired changes have been made. This difference is profound, and grasping it could save your marriage from unnecessary misery. Here's what I mean: You must abandon conditions when you marry.

I once heard a man who had been married more than thirty years say, "Our relationship has dramatically improved recently." "Why?" I asked. I was really curious. "I gave up all my expectations." As I pondered his words, I thought about how I have often withheld affection because Dori had not altered her behavior as I had hoped and had asked her to do. In other words, I was waiting for her to become a different person before giving her my love, rather than loving her as she was now. What if God treated us this way? We would all be lost, both now and forever!

That does not mean that we keep totally silent about our desires, or that we do not bring up matters that have arisen between us. Prompt and sincere communication is essential for a happy marriage. But once we have humbly expressed our requests—notice, I did not say *demands*—then we must resort

---

125 1 Pet 2:16–17.

to prayer and our own good example to influence our mate, but without any expectation of change. In other words, we resolve to love *this* person, not someone we hope he or she will become.

Humility and Forbearance

In Ephesians 4:1–2 we read, "I therefore, the prisoner of the Lord, beseech you to walk worthy of the calling with which you were called, with all lowliness and gentleness, with longsuffering, bearing with one another in love." One fundamental form of our new life in Christ, which is based on frank self-recognition, is humility. Knowing that I am a sinner saved by grace, I can look upon other believers in the same light. On the one hand, I am not surprised when either I or my spouse commits some awful sin. We do those things because, at least as far as our "old man"[126] is concerned, we are those kinds of people.

Armed with this awareness of myself and my wife, I can face the inevitable hurts that come to me from her hand, and tongue, and eyes, and actions. She is merely showing that she is a daughter of Eve, and my poor response reveals my Adamic descent. Far from reacting with anger or arrogant attack, I can now humbly see myself in her, as a fellow sinner, and see God's grace in her, as one forgiven through the blood of Jesus. Yes, she has wounded me deeply, and I feel the pain of it. She was wrong. I am, perhaps, outraged. But I am wrong, too. I have wronged her in similar ways, and I have wronged my God, whose Son loved me and gave himself for me. What right do I have to rise up in judgment upon her, or to harbor a grudge against her? I have been forgiven by God; shall I not respond to her as he has graciously responded to me, with patience, forbearance, and mercy?[127]

Such an attitude towards myself and my spouse frees me to offer full and complete pardon to her, even before she has fully comprehended the enormity of her "crime" (as I see it). Long before I came to myself and repented, God had sent his Son to suffer in my place; for decades, perhaps, he has patiently waited for me to

---

126 Eph 4:22; Col 3:9.
127 Eph 4:32.

recognize the horror of my unbelief, my selfishness, my stubborn refusal to bow in sorrowful contrition. He is slow to anger, quick to forgive the penitent supplicant for mercy; should I not be like him in this?

It works the other way, too. When my spouse expresses unhappiness with me, as a self-confessed sinner saved by grace, I am free to say, "You are right. I was wrong. Please forgive me." When I thus take her complaints seriously, without defending myself or questioning her right to evaluate my conduct or my character, then we have nothing about which to argue. We agree that I was wrong. We can move on now to prayer, asking God to forgive me and change me, and to give her grace to live with this miserable sinner whom God loves so much.

Friends, marriage can bring to you the most exquisite pleasure, but it will also inflict the most exquisite pain, caused by our indwelling sin. But God's grace is greater than all our sins! He has paid "double" for our wrongs in his son, Jesus Christ.[128] Where sin abounds, grace abounds all the more.[129] After we have admitted our offense and asked forgiveness from God and our spouse, we can resume our pilgrimage towards a new heaven and new earth, where we shall be fully righteous.[130] Furthermore, even before my wife has fully "confessed" her wrongs against me, I can imitate God and grant her full and complete remission, at least in my heart, and be set free from resentment.

Mutual Delight in God's Image

The differences between men and women need not simply be a source of frustration but are a special reflection of God's image and can be a blessing and means of sanctification. They are part of the variety that makes God's creation so wonderfully beautiful. If we will only study to understand the significant ways in which our spouse is not like ourselves, and then affirm these as gifts from God, we can then see beyond the routine annoyances

---

128 Isa 40:2.
129 Rom 5:20.
130 See Gal 5:5.

that sin produces, and either rejoice in our differences or laugh at them!

Because we are created in the image of God, we retain some of the glory of God in us, even though that beauty has been marred and obscured by the Fall. Our sin shows up in many ways, one of them being our failure to appreciate each other. Many couples swing wildly from mutual adoration during courtship to mutual disdain afterwards. One way to recapture the wonder and joy we once experienced is to decide to focus on our spouse's good qualities, those traits that attracted us to begin with. Yes, men and women are different, and these differences can drive us crazy, but they should also serve to curb our pride, our subjectivity, and our prejudice.

For example, many a husband is annoyed with his wife because of her tendency to repeat herself and to speak in hyperbole when she is upset. He asks himself, Why can't she just express her dissatisfaction calmly, once, and in clear prose? After about thirty years of this sort of frustration, I read *Men Are from Mars, Women Are from Venus*.[131] It came like a revelation to me: we really do communicate differently, and for different purposes! If a woman says, "You never help me around the house" she might really mean: "Right now, I feel that you are not giving me enough help."[132] "I don't have any friends!" might perhaps be interpreted as, "I am disappointed that Suzie seems to be too busy to spend time with me, even though she sees Alice regularly."

Still, I looked down upon her repetition and exaggeration, smug in my male rationality and precision of speech. Then one day, as I was reading the Bible, my proud little world was shattered. I suddenly realized that God sometimes talks like a woman! Read what Amos 5:21 records the Lord as saying: "I hate, I despise your feast days, and I do not savor your sacred assemblies." Can't you just hear the Israelites protest, "But LORD, you commanded us to offer these sacrifices!" Jeremiah's relentless criticisms of God's

---

131 John Gray, *Men are from Mars, Women are from Venus*. New York, NY: Harper, 2012.
132 I am speaking generally. Dori never actually said this.

people go on and on, and on, with considerable repetition and very little logical order. Why? Consider Jesus's denunciation of the Jewish religious leaders in Matthew 23. He keeps saying, "Woe to you..." Why couldn't he just tell them that they were self-righteous hypocrites, once, and let it go at that?

A few years ago, in a discussion about this with Dori and another woman, I said, "Why don't you just say it once, calmly?" She and her friend answered with one voice, "Because you don't get it the first time!" Here's the point: Women give vent to their unhappy feelings differently from the way men do, sometimes to our considerable annoyance. Rather than seeing this as a royal waste of time and energy, we should ask ourselves why they think they need to speak this way. Maybe I didn't hear her the first time. Perhaps my stubborn pride will not let me accept her legitimate complaints or criticisms. Could it be that God is speaking to me through her, and that he is also pretty upset with me?

Millions of wives feel a lack of emotional connection with their husbands, who don't seem to be hearing their heart concerns with attentive respect. Rather than dismissing what she says or jumping in with some "solution" to her problem, I ought to say something like, "I want to understand and feel your pain, but I'm not there yet. Can you tell me more?" And then I should simply listen!

Of course, we are all corrupted by the Fall, so our sin infects the way we say things. I am not here condoning angry, unfair, or unkind outbursts. What I believe we need to recognize, however, is that even when a woman repeats herself or uses hyperbole, she might be representing God, not only in what she says, but in how she says it. She is, after all, created in his image. It is worth noting as well that after I began to learn how to listen to Dori, she virtually stopped using those ways of communication that I found so hard to take. Maybe her repetition was provoked by my refusal to hear, and my hardness of heart was the cause of her hyperbole. In any case, rather than disdaining our spouse's differences, we should choose to appreciate and learn from them.

Recipients of Revelation

God has provided Christians not only comprehensive guidance on how to love each other, but complete assurance of his presence, power, provision, protection, and permanent love for them in Christ. From the first chapter of Genesis to the last words of Revelation, we see God's sovereign rule extending universally and eternally, the wise ways in which he leads his people, his tender care for us, and his ultimate purpose to conform us to the image of his son, Jesus.

When we are perplexed, therefore, we can turn to the Bible for guidance. Our inevitable failures will leave us feeling guilty, as they should, but the grace of God, which is available to all repentant sinners, will shine through our darkness and assure us of God's continued forgiveness. Aware of our inability to love one another as we love ourselves, we will receive encouragement from the promises of God's sufficient grace to fulfill his purposes for our lives, knowing that he will infuse us with the strength to break the bonds of our selfishness and even to sacrifice ourselves for one another. Sometimes, despite our best efforts, we shall be pierced with pangs of remorse, sorrow, and even grief, as our dreams for marriage crash upon the shoals of the intractable realities of our past and our present. In those moments of sadness and despair, we are assured that God is with us; that Jesus, the Man of Sorrows, knows our suffering; and that the Holy Spirit can assuage our wounds with his healing balm. The Bible will remind us that our hope is not to be fixed on this life, but on the grace to be brought to us at the revelation of Jesus Christ.[133]

Why, then, do so few Christians read their Bibles daily, much less study the Word of God, meditating upon it throughout the day, and committing its life-giving truths to memory? We cannot say that we don't have enough time, since we all make time for what we really want to do. Most folks do have the choice to turn off their television, computer, or phone, go into a quiet place, and listen attentively to what God has to say in the Scriptures. I know that mothers of young children may be utterly overwhelmed with the demands of their little ones, but they too can find ways

---

133 1 Pet 1:13.

to get the Word of God into their lives. Inscribing Bible verses on cards and putting them up some place where they can be seen easily throughout the day, listening to recordings of the Bible, and reading the Bible to their children (and thus to themselves) are a few examples. A considerate husband will make sure that his wife has at least a half hour each day to draw water from the wells of life through Bible reading and prayer.

Does the real problem lie in our own lack of spiritual hunger? Do we really want to know God, to love him, and to serve him in our married life? Or are we satisfied to sit before the television screen and be entertained by mostly worthless frivolity (at best)? Maybe we are simply too lazy to pick up the Bible. Some people have the mistaken idea that reading the Bible is work. I have found just the opposite to be the case: When I am really tired, or low, or feeling rushed, five minutes spent reading the Bible gives more "bang for the buck" than fifty minutes reading or watching anything else. Since 1965, the Bible has fed my soul, comforted my heart, renewed my mind, and clarified my perspective whenever I have opened its marvelous pages.

Not only do we have to spend private time attending to the Word of God in the Scriptures, but we also must make Bible reading a central feature of our life together as couples. This doesn't have to take a lot of time or require that the husband "preach" to his wife—far from it! For example, Dori and I simply read the appropriate passage from *Daily Light*, a collection of Scriptures for each day of the year, after supper at night.[134] This habit serves as a tether to our wandering hearts and distracted minds and draws us back to the source of all life, love, and peace.

Reading God's Word is a lifestyle, really. As Paul wrote, we should "let the word of Christ dwell [among us] richly in all wisdom, teaching and admonishing one another with songs and hymns and spiritual songs."[135] He probably had in mind what Moses

---

134 *Daily Light for Every Day*, with Anne Graham Lotz. Nashville, TN: Thomas Nelson, 1998, is one edition in the New King James Version. Many other editions of this old classic are available.

135 Col 3:16.

said to the people of Israel: "These words which I command you today shall be in your heart. You shall ... talk of them when you sit in your house, when you walk by the way, when you lie down, and when you rise up."[136] Church attendance helps to enforce this, for it enfolds us into the larger Christian community, and "forces" us to worship our great God and Savior at least once a week. Bible-based preaching both teaches us more about God's truth and challenges us to refashion our hearts and lives according to God's promises and precepts.

We are recipients of revelation! In the Scriptures, and especially in the words, works, and wonderful life of Jesus, we see God himself. He alone can set us free to love and to live with joy and hope, and he accomplishes this miracle chiefly through his own Word, as the Spirit of God engenders faith and obedience in us. There is no way I can sufficiently emphasize the necessity of opening our eyes, our minds, and our hearts to the words of God written in the Bible, both individually and together, if we want to enjoy the wonder-working power of God in our married life.

Responders to Revelation

Christian couples not only have the immense privilege of knowing God as he is revealed in the Bible, but also of drawing near to him in prayer. Our prayers to God properly flow from hearing what he has to say to us. That is, we first listen to God's voice, and then we speak. The old and almost trite adage, "The family that prays together, stays together," reflects a fundamental fact of marriage. We are not alone. Our relationship stands on the foundation of God's creation ordinance, by which man and woman were made for him and for each other, as well as for others. Living after the Fall, we are so impeded in our efforts to love each other that we absolutely must have God's help. Thankfully, God is more than happy to step into our lives and rescue us from ourselves and the messes we make.

Just as receiving God's revelation begins with, and requires, our own individual exposure to the Bible, so responding to his

---

136 Deut 6:6–7.

words of truth starts with each of us as individuals. All believers in Christ are God's beloved children, who have the inestimable authority to call him "Father," and who are invited to come into his presence as often as they want, assured of his affection and attention. So many promises about prayer fill the Scriptures that one can almost open any book and point your finger to the page, but Jesus' own guarantees must surely give us the most confidence that our Father in heaven will hear us when we pray.

One of Christ's most representative statements is found in John: "Whatever you ask the Father in My name he will give to you."[137] Of course, we need to understand what it means to ask in his name. Throughout the Bible, a person's name represents who that person is. So, to ask in Jesus' name is to come to the Father with requests based upon what Jesus has taught us, willing to follow in his example of sacrificial service and suffering, and being confident in his death and resurrection as the basis for our reconciliation and intimacy with God.

Jesus taught his disciples how to pray, using the words which we now know as the Lord's Prayer.

The version in Matthew 6:9–15 reads:

> Our Father in heaven
> Hallowed be Your name.
> Your kingdom come,
> Your will be done
> On earth as it is in heaven.
> Give us this day our daily bread.
> And forgive us our debts, as we forgive our debts.
> And do not lead us into temptation,
> But deliver us from the evil one [or, from evil].
> For Yours is the kingdom and the power and the glory
> forever. Amen.

This prayer, with the Jesus' added words about the necessity of forgiveness, gives us a profound yet simple model for

---

137 John 16:23.

our individual (and common) prayers.[138] We are to seek, first, God's name and fame, not our own; for his rule, not our own dominance; for his will to be done, not our own agenda. We may ask for our daily bread, which includes all that we need for bodily survival (though not most of the luxuries that most Americans have come to take for granted). When we plead for forgiveness, we imply that we are wrong, which is the case! In requesting his pardon, we refer him to the way in which we have forgiven others, including our spouse. Indeed, if we harbor resentment in our hearts against each other, Jesus states that we clearly do not have a relationship of grace with God. If we did, we would have extended to the other what he has so freely bestowed on us. As Paul writes, "Be kind to one another, tenderhearted, forgiving one another, even as God in Christ forgave you."[139] Our marriages will come under attack, both from our own sinful nature, as well as from temptations that assail us from the world around us and the evil machinations of the devil, so we beg God through the Lord's Prayer to keep us from falling into temptation and becoming captives to evil, knowing that we can't rely on our own strength. Eve tried that, as did Samson, and they both failed miserably.

In my experience, as I have prayed for my wife, God has answered, and worked miracles in her life. I now believe that the main thing I can do for her is to pray for her each day, specifically, and in the words of the Bible. When I am interceding for her, I often get ideas about how to love her; these are usually actions that speak her "love language" (which we will discuss in more detail later) and would not come naturally to me. I believe that the Lord plants those thoughts in my otherwise thick skull.

You could pray for your marriage in the following ways: Ask God to give you a supreme love for him as he is revealed in Jesus Christ, to fill your heart with his love, and to give you profound peace, based on his love and his care for all we need. He will provide! Ask God to help you to overcome your bad habits and frequent sins by showing you the root problem, which is usually

---

138 Matt 6:24-25.
139 Eph 4:32.

some false belief, and to give you self-control. Ask God to show you how your childhood has affected you, especially disappointment with parents, and to help you forgive your parents, even as you are honest about how you are disappointed with them or even still angry towards them. Ask him to show you how you are like your parents in their faults, and to change you. Ask him to give you a warm, forgiving spirit towards those who offend you, and to give you humility and patience, as he is patient towards us in our sin. Ask God to show you the deep inner needs of your spouse, and then give you grace to pray for him or her daily to be delivered from fear, anxiety, anger, resentment, envy, and covetousness, and to be filled with God's love.

Besides praying privately for your relationship, you should also come before God together in prayer daily. Dori and I do this twice a day: after breakfast, and after dinner. We simply bring before our Father the concerns each of us have and entrust them into his loving and powerful hands. We admit that we don't know what to do, or can't solve problems, or lack the strength to love. Over the past fifty years since we began this practice, we have found him to be utterly faithful, as he takes our weakness and ignorance and redeems us from our sins, to his glory and our good.

It's essential to establish this habit of daily prayer even before marriage, lest you drift into patterns that will be hard to break later. The man should take the lead, but if he doesn't, the woman should gently ask him to do so. If you are in a relationship with someone who refuses to pray with you, then do not expect your marriage to be filled with joy and love. I state it so starkly because I know how strong the forces are that conspire to deprive us of marital harmony, and how feeble we are to resist these on our own. I also know that God can overcome all obstacles to a loving marriage and to manifest his resurrection power in any situation where we humbly call upon him for help.

Leaving Parents: Repentance and Renewal

As we have seen, conflicts between husband and wife often

stem from a failure to "leave"[140] one's parents, either physically or emotionally. Peter says that we have been delivered from the "aimless conduct [futile ways] *received* by tradition from [our] fathers."[141] Jeremiah further defines these as "lies, worthlessness, and unprofitable *things*."[142] In other words, we must renounce the "ways"—habits, value systems, assumptions—of our parents, if these conflict with the Bible's teachings. Since all people, including our parents, suffer from the disease of sin, they will have passed on to us some bad habits, hurtful words, or inordinate affections that need to be discarded.

One of the best ways to discover these hidden sins in ourselves is to monitor our reaction to our spouse. What about your husband or wife irritates you most? What does he or she do that drives you wild with frustration, anger, or fear? Does this remind you of anything in your past? Does your spouse resemble one or both of your parents? Perhaps your intense negative reaction derives from resentment, disrespect, fear, or some other holdover from your childhood, and you are dumping all of that upon your poor spouse. Once, when I told my wife Dori that she was failing me in one particular fashion just as my father did, she said, "I am not your father!" She said pretty much the same thing when I remarked that she reminded me of my mother, and I wasn't talking about the lovable side of either one of them! Dori's point: It is not fair for me to unload upon her all the anger and longing that I have stored up inside me from my youth. She was right, of course.

What should you do when your spouse acts so much like your parents as to evoke all those ancient feelings? Part of making friends with God's purpose for our sanctification is to return to these wounds, re-open them, and ask God to deliver us from our sinful responses to our parents. First, we should admit to God how bad we still feel about what happened long ago. Then, rather than nursing grudges, wallowing in self pity, or clutching idols that

---

140 Gen 2:24.
141 1 Pet 1:18.
142 Jer 16:19.

we imagine will protect us from further harm, we can repent of our resentment and disrespect toward our parents, recognize our responsibility for how we live in the present, and renounce all inner vows or other false commitments that bind us to futility. After all, since God has forgiven you, how can you not forgive your parents? You can ask, also, for insight into what walls of defense you have built, or tactics for coping, even attack, you have adopted, to guard against further inner damage. These are really idols; you should instead be relying on God for protection and for the ability to love the unlovely. We must also ask God to show us whether any negative pronouncements about us remain in our minds, perhaps buried beneath layers of hurt and anger, and then ask him to set us free. We must use the Bible to replace error with truth. You are created in God's image. You are his beloved child. You can do all things through Christ who strengthens you.[143]

In all this process—and it is a journey that can take years, as the onion of your wounded soul is peeled, layer by layer—you can rejoice in God's patience towards you, his forgiveness of your wrongdoing, and his loving purpose to set you free from your inner child of the past. More than that, you can learn to see your spouse's irritating, and perhaps maddening, habits as your friends, sent by a loving Father to liberate you from futile old ways and enable you to live a life filled with new joy and power. We know that in this life we shall never receive total healing and freedom, so we rejoice in our hope of the resurrection, when we shall receive a glorified body and the Father himself will wipe away all our tears.

Even if we are not dealing with some "baggage" from our relationship with our parents, we still have to "leave" them, not only physically but also emotionally. That is, we need to transfer our primary allegiance from our father and mother to our spouse and make pleasing our spouse our chief priority – other than pleasing God, of course. Men must not look to their parents for financial help unless it is necessary, and women should be careful how they seek emotional support from their mothers. Of course, they will naturally turn to their mothers for understanding and

---

143 Phil 4:13.

advice, but they should refrain from complaining about their husbands. Without going into detail, they can simply express how they are feeling and ask for prayer to respond in a godly way.

That doesn't mean that we cut off all communication with them. Far from it. We shall want to talk with them in one way or another, as often as possible, as long as this does not nurture a dependence upon them.

Cleaving to Your Spouse

Just as leaving is both physical and emotional, so is cleaving. Clinging to one's marriage partner includes living together, emotional and mental closeness, physical intimacy, and a shared spiritual life. Physical nearness is essential to a healthy marriage. Today's growing tendency for spouses to live in different cities to pursue further studies, separate careers, or even Christian ministry spells trouble for marital intimacy. Even long separations should be ruled out.

Not only should couples live together, but they must also spend time together each day. Emotional, mental, and spiritual "clinging" is necessary for our love to grow. This means really listening to one another, drawing near in honest and personal communication, truly trying to understand, and even "getting into" the other's mind and heart. As spouses share their daily experiences, talk (kindly) about their friends and work, express their shared concerns, and discuss common projects, the bond between them is strengthened.[144] Over time, such shared memories become a key component of the glue that binds them so tightly to each other. Spiritual closeness will not be possible unless the Bible is read aloud regularly, so that life together is framed by, and founded upon, the truth of God's revelation. Worship in church and at home, including prayer for one another and with one another, will weave a cord that is not easily broken.

Cleaving to your spouse also includes touching, eye contact,

---

144 Paul Tournier, *To Understand Each Other* not only shows the immense importance of seeking simply to understand each other, but also teaches us how to overcome barriers to mutual understanding. I highly recommend this brief classic.

sleeping together, and sexual relations. Without this sort of bodily intimacy, a marriage can't thrive, and may even wither and die. Why is a normal sexual relationship so important? Tim LaHaye, in *The Act of Marriage*, gives many reasons, including the release of tension, promotion of overall health and well-being, deepening of intimacy, and new life in the form of children.[145] These little ones, in turn, further strengthen the bond between husband and wife, as they see each other in their children and as they seek to bring them up together. As St. Paul pointed out long ago, frequent sexual relations also help to stem the onslaught of temptation from outside.[146]

Regular and loving sexual relations will require time; commitment; good health; mutual forgiveness based on open, frequent, and honest communication; genuine love for each other; skill and knowledge; and especially prayer. God created sex and wants married people to enjoy and love each other in this way, but so many forces conspire to deprive us of one of life's chief joys that we must call upon his help in prayer, both separately and together. Husbands must be sensitive to timing and mood and must create an atmosphere of spiritual and emotional closeness, including tender words and frequent kisses and embraces of a non-erotic nature, to surround their wives with a sense of being loved. Wives need to try to be attractive, available, and receptive to their husband's advances. If a woman is sick or upset, then she should explain that to her husband, lest he think that he is being rejected. Remember that physical affection is one of his major languages of love; he is not just after your body but is seeking intimacy with his spouse.[147]

This clinging must be to the exclusion of all others. To be joined to one's spouse implies that we are not bound up with our

---

145 Tim LaHaye and Beverly LaHaye, *The Act of Marriage: The Beauty of Sexual Love*. (Grand Rapids: MI: Zondervan, 1998).

146 1 Cor 7:2.

147 Specific instructions on how to engage in satisfying sexual intercourse may be found in a number of books, notably Ed Wheat's *Sex Life for Every Married Couple*.

parents, work and careers, children, and definitely not another man or woman. Not that we don't attend to our parents and children and work, or that we have no friends of the opposite sex, but that we do not become so involved with them, or spend so much time on them, that our mental and emotional focus is diverted from our spouse, who deserves much more of our attention than anyone or anything else.

Reducing the risks of adultery

"You shall not commit adultery."[148] This clear command comes into our fantasy-land romance with brutal honesty. The love which seems so beautiful, if acted upon, constitutes a clear violation of God's moral law. "But," you say, "I don't mean to carry this all the way to consummation. I just want to share my heart, not my bed, with this person. Can't we talk with each other and enjoy what is obviously a unique and very satisfying emotional kinship?" When Jesus said that an intentionally lustful look amounts to adultery in the heart, he showed that, as Proverbs says, you must "keep your heart with all diligence, for out of it *spring* the issues of life."[149] Not only can thoughts lead to actions; they *are* actions, mental acts that can bind us to another person even while creating an inner distance from our spouse. That is why we must rein in our imaginations and daydreams as well as our words.

"Love your neighbor as yourself"[150] gives us positive direction. How would I want my spouse to handle a strong attraction for someone else? That becomes the standard by which I should rule myself. This simple principle rules out private, personal, or frequent communication, not to mention physical contact, with anyone other than our spouse (or family members). No one will say that it is easy to deny yourself the pleasure of sharing at least part of your life with someone whom you really love, even if he or she is not your spouse. We may complain that there are too many unfulfilled desires in our hearts, too many aching gaps in our

148 Ex 20:14.
149 Prov 4:23.
150 Mk 12:31.

existing marriages. God created us for intimacy, and our restless souls will pursue that for which we were made, even if we are grabbing for forbidden fruit.

"If your right eye causes you to sin, pluck it out and cast *it* from you ... if your right hand causes you to sin, cut it off and cast *it* from you."[151] Jesus meets our desperate searching for intimacy with a brutal demand: Make war on anything that might lead you into sin. He gives the reason: "It is more profitable that one of your members perish, than for your whole body to be cast into hell." In other words, adultery, if not repented of and forsaken, can lead to eternal destruction in hell. Better to suffer severe "amputation" now than to be plunged into the lake of fire forever. Paul puts it another way: "Flee sexual immorality"[152]—that is, any illicit action or relationship outside of marriage.

Practically, that might mean that we must cut off all private communication, by phone, email, texting, or face-to-face conversation. We must avoid situations where we might encounter him or her alone, or occasions which might tempt us to revive our passion. We must put away mementoes and reminders that might light the flame again.

Positively, we should do all we can to draw near to God. He understands. We can pour out our lonely sighs to him, begging for his love to fill the holes that we all have in our hearts. As we seek intimacy with him, his love for us seeps into our souls and satisfies in a way that no one else can. We also need to expend every effort to re-build our relationship with our spouse, which has probably suffered at least neglect, and perhaps worse, during our preoccupation with someone else. Will this be easy? No! Will drastic measures ensure that our own marriage will ever live up to our earlier expectations? Possibly not. Will we avoid a great deal of heartache for ourselves and others if we refuse to give in to our love for another person and marshal all our energies to love our own spouse? Yes!

Lest you think that "cleaving" to someone or something

151 Matt 5:29–30.
152 1 Cor 6:18.

other than your spouse is not a danger for you, it might be good to ask, What really excites you? What fills your daydreams? When you have free time, how do you spend it? What do you ask for in prayer? Who are the people with whom you most enjoy spending time? If the answer to any of these questions reveals a mental or emotional attachment that rivals, or even eclipses, your attraction for your spouse, then take that as a warning signal. While I do not mean that our lives should be totally wrapped up in our marriage—that can be a form of idolatry—we must not ignore the force of the word "cleave." It means to cling to, adhere to, stick to, or be entwined with. Aside from the obvious reference to the act of marriage, this term points us towards the unique tie that binds a man and his wife.

If our recreation, work, service to church or community, or even care for our children hinders us from focusing on our spouse, then something is wrong. Take our use of time, for example. Marriage counselor Willard Harley has discovered that American men spend about fifteen hours a week courting the woman they hope to marry.[153] When he advises them to invest an equivalent amount of time with their wives after marriage, these same men look at him in disbelief. Clearly, having gained their objective, they think that can, and should, move on to other things. Their wives, on the other hand, may feel abandoned, even betrayed, by the man who used to be in such ardent pursuit of them. We are, of course, to give God our hearts first and foremost, but after that, our hearts should be filled with thought and care and kind concern for our spouse. The lack of such a concentration upon our marriage partner lies at the root of much sorrow and separation today.

Loving Leadership

God commands husbands to lead their wives as Christ leads the church.[154] They have been given authority, yes, but they must exercise it not in a worldly fashion but following the

---

153 Willard Harley, *His Needs, Her Needs*. (Revised edition. (Grand Rapids, MI: Revell, 2011).
154 Eph 5:25-33.

footsteps of Jesus. As leader of his wife, the husband should seek her welfare. First and foremost, he seeks her spiritual welfare, like Christ, who first gave himself for the church and now engages in the daily work of sanctifying her, that is, making her holy, set apart for God's glory.[155] Of course, we husbands cannot give ourselves as a sacrifice for our wives' salvation—that has been done, once for all, by Jesus—but we can imitate his example of self-giving in order to promote their relationship with God. This thought has challenged me many times and lassoed me back from selfishness. It really helps me to have the goal of helping my wife to know and love God better. Rather than seeking my own interests, I should be asking the Lord for grace to lead her closer to him.

Specifically, in addition to praying for her and leading her in Bible reading and prayer together, I should try to provide her with a living example of humility, self-emptying, and service.[156] Am I speaking to build my wife up in faith, hope, and love? Do I lead her in activities that will encourage her to trust God and imitate the example of Jesus? My suggestions for entertainment, friends, and leisure time, for example, will refct just how much I make her relationship with God my first priority.

If she sees me forgiving her as God forgives me,[157] God's grace to her is being presented in visible, audible form. As I make it clear that growth in holiness stands at the top of my "to do" list, then she will be challenged to follow my lead in seeking after God before all else. When I gently remind her of God's promises and of his precepts for living, she will have more resources to resist the temptations that the rest of her world throws at her daily. My words of praise for her virtues and her attempts to obey God will spur her on to continue on that lonely path. If I deny myself in order to know and serve God, she will see the work of the Spirit of Christ in me. Maybe it is just a matter of eating less, or exercising more, or turning off the television, or putting down the games, or calling a discouraged friend. A willingness to serve in church, or to

---

155 Eph 5:25–26.
156 See Phil 2:1–11 for the way that Paul works this out.
157 Eph 4:32.

help a neighbor, and especially my commitment to train and care for the children, will demonstrate to her what living for God and for others really looks like.

We are all fallen creatures, however, and we husbands are no exception. That is why one of the most "sanctifying" things we can do for our wives is to admit our mistakes, apologize, and ask for forgiveness. Don't worry about losing her respect if you own up to your failures. She knows about them anyway and will only respect you more if you agree with her about your shortcomings. That doesn't mean that you have to tell her every time you lust after another woman or visit a pornographic web site. Such knowledge might be too much for her to handle, and is best disclosed to your spiritual partner, another man with whom you share your struggles to follow Christ. I'm not endorsing voyeurism, by any means! But the faults I think we should confess to our wives are those actions, and inactions, that they see and that cause them grief. Our confession should be frank, simple, and without any excuses (such as, "I was just too tired"; "I was hungry"; "I was under a lot of stress"). In other words, we should not only be leaders in piety and holiness, but in repentance.

We might need help with this. We are often so blind to our own faults, and busy with our many pursuits, that we just don't know what we are doing that does not bring glory to God or resemble Jesus. On rare occasions, I have asked Dori in what ways I need to grow, and her answers have always been stunningly quick and perceptive. Clearly, she had been thinking about this for a while, and knew just what to say when I gave her an opening.

I do not have to emphasize what stands out with brilliant clarity as a luminous background to all that I have been saying: In order to imitate Christ, we must know him. If I am going to set before my wife an example of Christ-like behavior, I need to be thinking about him, reading about him, speaking to him, and asking for the Holy Spirit to re-enact the life, death, and resurrection of Jesus in and through me. Furthermore, I won't be able to admit my sins to her unless I have first taken them to God in full repentance and firm faith in his grace and mercy. Only as I have drunk from the wells of salvation will I be able to humble myself before the person who means most to me, and whose admiration, affection, and acceptance I so desperately crave. Thus, our first duty as husbands is to know Christ, to lean on him, to seek his face and his strength, to rest in his love for us, and to ask for his power to follow in his footsteps of sacrificial love.[158]

Having described the headship of the husband, Paul goes on to say that the husband should love his wife as he loves his own body, which he nourishes and cherishes.[159] A wise and loving husband sees his wife as part of himself. He thinks about her welfare, plans for her personal prosperity as much as for his own, provides for her, and protects her. Even if she has to have a job, he sees himself as the one primarily responsible for her physical nurture. Instead of irritating her with the sight of an inactive husband when she is feeling overworked, he cheerfully responds to requests for help and seeks out practical ways to serve her. By opening the door for her, he expresses his tender care. If he knows she is coming home with a heavy load of groceries, he stands ready at the door to help her carry them into the house. He asks constantly, "How can I help you?" He invites her to take him into her life by asking questions about her day. He listens attentively when she wants to talk late at night when all he wants is either sleep or sex. Rather than making light of her fears, he takes them seriously, while still encouraging her to trust God and assuring her that he will be there to take care of her. Although he may find some of her preoccupations a bit strange—such as the way her hair looks, or what color the bridesmaids' dresses should be, or what present to give to Aunt Clara – he will try his best to see things from her standpoint rather than belittling her or brushing her off.

Just as men are to lead and love their wives, they are also to support their wives in their unique challenges as women. Peter instructs, "Husbands, likewise, dwell with *them* with understanding, giving honor to the wife, as to the weaker vessel, and as *being* heirs

158 1 Pet 2:21–24.
159 Eph 5:28–29.

together of the grace of life."[160] Being equally created in the image of God, and equally saved by grace through faith in Christ, wives are as capable and worthy as their husbands in the most fundamental ways. In their femininity, however, women are weaker than men.

Besides obvious physical generalities such as height and muscle mass, women are "weaker" because they are subject to hormonal fluctuations that do not affect men. Their hormones influence their whole body, as well as their emotions, especially at particular times, such as before and during the monthly menstrual period, pregnancy, after giving birth, and menopause. The intensity of impact varies greatly from woman to woman, and is determined by heredity, environment, childhood, diet, physical fitness, mental health, spiritual vitality, and many other factors. Some students of human behavior link a very serious problem with pre-menstrual syndrome (PMS) to a rejection of one's femininity, perhaps stemming from a mother's bad example or a father's disappointment at not having a son. If your wife struggles with PMS, you might explore this possibility with her and pray with her for deliverance, but only at a time to which you have both agreed, and when she is calm enough to do so.

At such times, ignorant and foolish is the man who belittles his wife's struggles to maintain emotional equilibrium or to handle routine physical tasks with her usual control. What your wife needs then is understanding, not ridicule or neglect. Take time to listen to her, patiently and without trying to correct what seems to you to be a skewed evaluation of things. Let her know that you care and that you are ready to drop everything to help her out. Too many of us husbands have taken complaints or criticisms personally, when these are merely the overflow of a distressed mind that has temporarily lost perspective. She may indeed be irritated with you for past or present failures to care for her, but she probably doesn't hate you, though she may talk and act that way! More likely, she is frustrated by her inability to cope as usual and is perhaps angry with herself. At the same time, these indictments, though perhaps exaggerated a bit, and thus quite hard to take without defending

---

160 1 Pet 3:7.

oneself, usually contain more than a grain of truth. They are God's wake-up call to get our minds off our work or play for a while and focus on our wife's need for our undivided attention and affection. If we denigrate their fears or deny our failures, we are just digging a deeper pit of despair for our wives, and thus for ourselves.

Many women also experience general depression. Although turning to anti-depressant drugs may seem necessary for a while to treat serious depression, these pills are potent and have many side effects, including loss of libido and weight gain, which can make matters worse by putting a damper on normal sexual relations. They also may cause severe mental and emotional reactions.[161] Even if it appears that a woman is really in danger of deep depression, I would suggest that other avenues be explored, including regular exercise, a healthier diet, adequate sunshine, constant and tender care by her husband, and prayer for God to heal any inner wounds. Seek the help of another woman to whom your wife can speak frankly, and who will understand as no man can.

Here I must add a strong word of caution: There is an almost universal tendency for wives to talk about their husbands' flaws to other women, who frequently give them unconditional sympathy. Even if what she says is true, for a wife to reveal her husband's faults and weaknesses to others is to fail to show him respect. The Bible tells us to take our complaints to people directly, not go to others behind their backs.[162] Spreading ill reports about another, especially if they are exaggerated or one-sided, is called either gossip or slander, and the Bible calls both serious sins.[163] In particular, the Bible warns women not to indulge in this sort of conduct.[164] We all know that a "secret" a wife shares about her husband will probably be passed on to others, further ruining his reputation among her friends.

---

161 For other risks, see http://www.cchrint.org/psychiatric-drugs/antidepressantsideeffects/

162 Lev19:15-16; Matt 18:15-17.

163 On gossip and being a tale-bearer, see Prov 20:19; Rom 1:29; 2 Cor 12:20. On slander, see Ps 50:20; 101:5; Prov 10:18; 16:28; Mk 7:22; Rom 1:30; 2 Cor 12:20; 2 Tim 3:3; Eph 4:31; 1 Pet 2:1.

164 1 Tim 3:11; 5:13; Tit 2:3.

You may by all means tell your friend that you get angry and sad, and that it's hard sometimes to show respect to your husband, but do not spill his secrets or give the impression that he is the *cause* of your troubles when he is only the *occasion* of them.

Sometimes, a wife must tell someone else about her husband's behavior, if he is violently abusive, alcoholic, or addicted to drugs. If either spouse, including the wife, has spoken kindly and frankly to the other about behavior that is highly offensive and hurtful, and the response has not been good, then an outside person – preferably someone trained in mediating disputes – should be called in. No one, especially a woman, should be subjected to prolonged stress caused by extreme mistreatment.

The Armed Forces Officer, a manual for officers, says that "Rank should be used to serve one's subordinates." My father, who was a Naval officer, told me frequently, "The ship comes first. In the Army, the company comes first. See that the men have eaten before you eat; don't lie down to sleep until you are sure they are taken care of. Rise early to be there when they wake up." If these principles hold true for the military, how much more should husbands exemplify self-sacrificial service at home! The Prayer of St. Francis reminds us to seek to love rather than be loved, understand rather than be understood, give rather than to receive, all of these coming straight from the pages of the Gospel portrait of Christ:

> *Lord, make me an instrument of Your peace.*
> *Where there is hatred, let me sow love;*
> *where there is injury, pardon;*
> *where there is doubt, faith;*
> *where there is despair, hope;*
> *where there is darkness, light;*
> *where there is sadness, joy.*
>
> *O Divine Master, grant that I may not so much seek*
> *to be consoled as to console;*
> *to be understood as to understand;*
> *to be loved as to love;*

For it is in giving that we receive;
it is in pardoning that we are pardoned;
it is in dying that we are born again to eternal life.

Jesus said, "For their sakes I sanctify Myself, that they also may be sanctified by the truth."[165] As his followers, we husbands should progress in making humble Christ-likeness our principal goal, so that our wives might learn from our example. Paul put it in a slightly different way: "I endure all things for the sake of the elect, that they also may obtain the salvation which is in Christ Jesus with eternal glory."[166] He was willing to suffer, if only others might be saved. This is our challenge, men: sanctification, suffering, and service. A husband who earnestly pursues these goals will probably find that his wife is ready to follow him with great affection.

Submission

"Wives, likewise, *be* submissive to your own husbands."[167]

While men are called to lead their wives, women are called to submit to their husbands. What does it mean for a wife to submit? At the very least, she should obey her husband's decisions for their common life, including the upbringing of their children. "But what if he is wrong? How can I submit to him if his decisions are not right?" First, we must say that when a wife goes along with her husband because she thinks he is correct, that is not submission, but agreement. It's precisely when we do not agree with those in authority that we must choose to obey them rather than to rebel.

This does not mean that a wife cannot express her opinion and humbly urge her husband to reconsider, nor that a wise man should not take his wife's opinion very seriously, and hold off from executing any plan to which she really objects until he has prayed further, sought counsel from godly men (and perhaps women), and tried very hard to understand what she is saying. Furthermore, there may be times when the husband's proposed

---

165 John 17:19.
166 2 Tim 2:10.
167 1 Pet 3:1. See also Eph 5:22–24; Col 3:18; Tit 2:5.

decision seems to his wife to be either clearly against Scripture or harmful to herself or the children. If that happens, and if she has already spoken to him without effect, then she is warranted in asking some other man, perhaps an elder in the church or the pastor, to help them communicate about the matter. If there is risk of imminent danger, she may even have to call someone to come and intervene, including – as a last resort – the police. After she has done her best to persuade her husband, however, he must take responsibility for setting policy, and she must humbly comply with his decision, trusting in God to work all things together for her good.

Submission also involves showing respect at all times,[168] even when your husband does not earn such treatment. Women often find it especially difficult to admire a man who doesn't love them. What they need to remember, however, is that respect includes both inner appreciation and outer expression. Even if she doesn't fully admire her husband, a wife can, and should, express respect toward him in speech, countenance, and actions. She can do this in a variety of ways. Negatively, she can avoid frequent criticism, correction, and other indications that she considers him incompetent or ill-willed. Positively, she can choose to commend him for his abilities and achievements, being specific so that he will know she means it. She will be surprised by how much just a little affirmation will change his attitude towards her.

Even if her husband does not improve, however, a submissive wife can know that she has obeyed God and that her gentle and quiet spirit is extremely beautiful and precious in God's eyes.[169] Her calm and cooperative response to her husband will express her faith and hope in God, even if she cannot fully trust her husband to do what is best for her or the family. Peter gives the example of Sarah, Abraham's long-suffering wife, who had to put up with a man who twice betrayed her in order to save his own skin.[170] She will also enjoy the benefits of a clear conscience, and of

---

168 Eph 5:33.
169 1 Pet 3:4
170 1 Pet 3:5-6

the reduction of conflict in her marriage, since she has refused to disobey her husband and has chosen to follow the path of peace, which leads to blessing.[171] In the unlikely event that she actually suffers verbal abuse or violence in response to her godly conduct, she will know that Jesus walked that arduous road long before her, and fully understands how it feels.[172] Watching their mother, her children will learn priceless lessons of Christian discipleship.

Once again, however, I must make it clear that I do not condone verbal or physical abuse by men against their wives or children. If she or the children are in danger of harm, a wife has a duty to remove herself and them from danger and to report his violent actions to others, starting with the male family members, then leaders in the church, and then the police. At no time should she allow herself or her children to be kept in a position of real risk.

Reclaiming Fruitfulness and Dominion

Since physical wellness affects both our ability to carry out our work and be a good sexual companion, giving attention to this area in our own lives shows our spouse that we want to be the best we can be for them. Making our spouse's health a priority (in a supportive rather than a nagging way) shows our care for his or her personal happiness and vitality. As the years add up, physical health takes on added importance. You can only slow the inevitable loss of strength and vitality that comes with getting older by building a lifetime of sound habits. These include getting at least seven hours of sleep a night, preferably eight hours, eating a healthy diet with lots of fruits, vegetables, and whole grains, exercising at least thirty minutes each day (preferably more—much of which can consist of hard cleaning around the house, washing the car, tending the yard, etc.), and avoidance of things that aren't good for you, such as drugs, cigarettes, and excessive alcohol.

"Bearing fruit" also includes, obviously, bringing children into the world. Truly, "Children are a heritage from the LORD."[173]

---

171 1 Pet 3:8-12
172 1 Pet 3:13-18
173 Ps 127:3

They bring great joy into our lives and enable us to grow in maturity as persons and as Christians. As we seek to "bring them up in the training and admonition of the Lord,"[174] we ourselves are formed more nearly into the image of Christ. Their trials and troubles touch our hearts to the core and drive us to God in prayer and faith. We realize that we need to set a good example for them, so we try to eliminate bad habits and acquire better ones. Years of investment in their lives will "pay off" as we see them grow up into godly men and women, as they take on responsibilities in life, and as they bring new offspring into the world. Together, as a family we learn to "take dominion" over the house, the yard (if we have one), all our possessions, as well as our time. Later, these children will in turn exercise Christian dominion in ways that bring blessing to those around them.

Communicating Love

Gary Chapman, in *The Five Love Languages*, says that we each "speak" a "primary love language."[175] There are, he claims, five of these: words of affirmation, quality time, giving and receiving gifts, acts of service, and physical touch. Of course, we all appreciate all of these, but one of them will be especially important to us, so much so that if we don't "hear" the other speaking in this language, we will not easily believe that we are really loved. That means that you need to understand your primary love language and that of your spouse and be sure to communicate in a way that each can understand. For example, my primary language seems to be quality time, followed by words of affirmation. Dori, however, seems to value acts of service and giving and receiving gifts. Since Dori does not share my primary love language, I must ask God for wisdom about how to love her. If your spouse does not "speak" your language well, you can tell him or her how you like to be loved, but you also need to see how hard it is going to be, and not expect him or her to pick up a new language without a great

---

174 Eph 6:4.

175 Gary Chapman, *The Five Love Language*. (Chicago, IL: Northfield Publishing, 2015).

deal of effort and time. So, just try to be patient, and put your expectations wholly upon God, who *does* know how to speak your primary love language!

Although we may communicate in a variety of unspoken ways, we need to pay special attention to how we communicate with our words. You can't have a successful marriage without asking for, and granting, forgiveness. But there is something else you can do that will greatly reduce the need to forgive each other: speak words of life. A few years ago, I became aware that I was not speaking enough encouraging words to Dori, so I began to make a "project" out of increasing the number of positive things I said to her. It was a bit awkward at first, even for me, but soon I found that I was actually *looking* for good things to say to her. Like all women, Dori possesses many fine qualities, and does countless acts of goodness for me and for others. All I had to do was to take note of these and mention them to her. Words of life can also encompass simple courtesy, such as smiling and saying, "please," and, "thank you." After less than a year, this became habitual for me, and I found that she was responding in kind. Our conversations are now laced with much more expressions of appreciation, making for a very amicable relationship.

Something else happened that really surprised me: My words began to influence my thoughts. There was a time in my life, of which I am terribly ashamed, when you could ask me whether Dori had any faults and I would reel off a long list of them without having to pause to think. Now it's just the opposite: I would have to stop and ponder a while to come up with more than a few shortcomings. It is not that she is perfect, but that my mind has taken another turn, and I travel a different mental road, surrounded on either side with fair flowers of gratitude for her. The tongue has awesome power.[176] We can utter words of life or sentences of death. Despite the one major improvement I just mentioned, I have recently become aware of just how destructive, or at least non-constructive, my speech has been over the past

---

176 See Jas 3:1–12 for a penetrating description of the damage that our speech can inflict.

five decades with Dori. More times than I could count, I have said things that do not express the three most important things we should always affirm: faith, hope, and love.

Faith: That God is with us; that he will guide and provide; that he forgives all our sins; that he will renew us daily if we turn to him; that he will never leave us nor forsake us; that nothing can separate us from his love for us in Christ Jesus.[177]

Hope: That God will cause all things to work together for good for those who love him; that he will "restore to you the years that the swarming locust has eaten"[178]; that he will raise us up, with glorified bodies, to enjoy a new heaven and a new earth, where righteousness dwells. If our hope is fixed fully on the grace that is to be brought to us at the revelation of Jesus Christ, we shall be able to bear the inevitable disappointments and even grief that mark this world of sorrows.[179]

Love: Love for God, who has given us his only Son as a redemption for our sins;[180] for Jesus, who gave himself for us;[181] for each other, despite our many faults and failings; for other believers in Christ; love for others, even those who mistreat us; for the billions of souls who do not yet know God through faith in Christ.

To put it in another way, we should speak to build each other up, as Paul wrote: "Let no corrupt [unwholesome, rotten] word proceed out of your mouth, but what is good for necessary edification, that it may impart grace to the hearers."[182] That is, we should not open our mouths in order to express ourselves, but to encourage others. Our aim in speaking should be to inject health, life, and light into the other person's thoughts and feelings, rather than corruption, death, and darkness. That doesn't mean that we preach to each other all the time, or much of the time at all, but that we take care to say things that are both true and loving;

---

177 Matt 6:33; 1 John 1:9-10; 2 Cor 3:18; Heb 13:5; Rom 8:39.
178 Rom 8:28; Joel 2:25; Phil 3:20-21; 2 Pet 13.
179 1 Pet 1:13.
180 John 3:16.
181 Gal 2:20.
182 Eph 4:29.

things that put a different, and more positive, perspective on a difficult situation, that direct our minds and thoughts to God, his love, and his power.

Sometimes, however, silence, coupled with inner prayer, is golden, and just what the other really requires at that moment. Indeed, learning to listen may be the most important communication skill of all. Something we want to say might be, in principle, heartening and up-building, but our partner may not be in the mood to hear it, or it may not suit his or her need. Careful listening must precede caring words, lest we cause damage rather than create hope. Gentle questions ("How did that make you feel?") and affirming comments ("You seem to be quite upset by this") often work much better than advice or exhortations, not to mention negative comments ("If you had only... then this wouldn't have happened!"). The Apostle James wrote, "Be swift to hear, slow to speak, slow to wrath."[183] By allowing the other to speak, we communicate respect—a respect based upon a conviction that our spouse is made in the image of God and has God-given value as a human being. Keeping quiet while the other talks indicates that we affirm his or her intelligence, legitimate desires, and natural responses to both positive and painful stimuli. By not jumping in to advise or to moralize, we are saying that we have a high regard for what he or she is thinking, feeling, and saying, even if we don't agree.

If our tongues would be filled with praise and thanksgiving to God, appreciation and affection for each other, and kindness for everyone else, then our homes would be wrapped in an aura of joy and peace. In addition to these life-giving words, we need to make kind gestures. Offer to give your spouse a back rub to soothe tired muscles after a long day. Cook your husband's favorite meal. Bring home some flowers for your wife. Once you start seeking tangible ways to show love, you may find yourself enjoying being a person filled with affection instead of resentment or hurt or just indifference. Who knows? Your spouse may someday repay you with similar kindnesses; maybe not. Remember that we are not

---

183 Jas 1:19.

fishing for anything in return, but merely seeking to be kind; to give, not to get.[184] Regardless of the other's response, you will stop (or prevent) the creeping desert of discontent that threatens to destroy everything that has life.

Confronting Conflict, Denying Divorce, and Seeking Help

When two sinners live together, they are bound to irritate each other. We are just too different from one another— our family background, personality, interests, experiences, and fundamental gender dissimilarities. All these, plus the pressures of daily life, will lead to unpleasant encounters, disagreements, and disappointment. Rather than running away from the pain that comes from conflict, however, we could choose to embrace this as an opportunity to grow.

The key thing is to communicate. Set a weekly time to talk about anything you want to, but especially anything that you might have done, or not done, to hurt each other. Do your utmost not to have these discussions either on an empty stomach or just before bed. Shortly after dinner may be the best time, or after the kids have gone to bed. Each person can have the same amount of time to express dissatisfaction, while the other listens and takes notes, or perhaps asks questions for clarification only. Then the other can do the same. Stay calm, if possible; don't interrupt, deny what the other says, or retaliate with counter-charges. Try to understand before speaking. Explain what seems to be unclear or incorrectly perceived. If you wronged your spouse, apologize. Say, "You are right. I was wrong. I am sorry. Please forgive me." The proper response to that is, "Thank you for saying that. I do forgive you."

If you are very angry about something that happened during the day, then you shouldn't wait to say so. You don't have to go into all the details. Just say, "When you did that, I felt angry, and I still haven't settled down. Please pray for me." Notice that the focus is on how you feel, not on how awfully you think you have been treated. Keep it simple; you don't need to launch into

---

184 "It is more blessed to give than to receive," Acts 20:35.

a bitter recital of all previous wrongs, for these should have been dealt with at the time, or in your weekly "conference."

Try not to ascribe motives: "I know you don't care about how I feel, or you would have…" You probably don't know what is in the other person's mind. Just describe your reaction to his or her actions. That will make it easier to comprehend and to discuss. When your mate mentions something like this to you, take it as vital information. Either she is right, or she is wrong. If she is right, you need to repent, apologize, and ask God to forgive and change you. If he is wrong, you need to know how he looks at things. Perhaps, in time, you can either alter your behavior or explain what you are doing in to clear up misunderstandings.

What happens, you may ask, when my best efforts don't bring results? Do I give up and walk out? Give God time to change the other person as you do what is right. Even if no change comes, we must look to God to reward us. Emerson Eggerichs states, "Ultimately, your spouse and your marriage have nothing to do with it. You are simply demonstrating your obedience and trust in the face of an unlovable wife or an unrespectable husband. *Unconditional love and unconditional respect will be rewarded.*"[185]

Before we were married, Dori and I agreed that divorce would never be an option for us. That was not just because God hates divorce,[186] but because we knew that if we thought we could always get out of our marriage, we would not do our utmost to make it work. That resolve has given us a firm place to stand over the decades, for we have always tried to deal with our conflicts rather than give up and renounce our wedding vows. A more detailed discussion of divorce and remarriage can be found in the appendices.

You may find that some conflicts are just too difficult to settle by yourselves. Wives especially come to this conclusion rather quickly and try to get their husbands to see a marriage counselor with them. The husband, being a man, would rather solve the problem himself than ask for help, so he typically resists

---

185 Eggerichs, *Love & Respect*, 271.
186 Mal 2:16,

his wife's urgings. As someone who has been the recipient of about a dozen years of marriage counseling over three decades, I would recommend that you do see a counselor if you have tried everything I have suggested and still cannot discuss your negative feelings together without getting into an argument, or without one of you (usually the wife) feeling that the other is simply not getting the point.

If you do seek counseling, you should find a Christian counselor, perhaps a pastor or a layperson with special training. The counselor's primary responsibility is to referee your conversation; help clarify misunderstandings; and prod one or the other to listen, reflect, and express his or her reactions calmly and courteously. If the husband and wife are both immature spiritually, then the counselor will have to remind them of the sort of basic Christian truths and marital principles included in this handbook.

Perseverance and Hope in God

Don't give up! Remember that marriage, like all of life, is intended by God for our sanctification, and that this process is often compared to a refining fire.[187] God wants to burn away the dross and impurities of your old self and recreate a new person in the image of Christ. To do so, he may have to resort to severe measures. Make friends with these, cooperate with God in his kind purpose for you, rely on the Holy Spirit, and you will see substantial change over a period of a few years.

At least, you will know that you are changing. Your spouse may not grow as fast you would like; in fact, I can almost guarantee that. But you can draw closer to Christ, learn more of how he suffered at the hands of sinners, and gradually be able to resemble him in his humility, patience, and forbearing love. To be like Christ, in fact, is our primary purpose in life.[188] How can we do this without going through some of what he suffered? So, hang in there! God is with you and will never leave you nor forsake you.[189]

187 See 1 Pet 1:6-7.
188 Rom 8:29; 1 Jn 2:6; 3:2.
189 Hebrews13:5.

More than that, he will show up, surprising you with answers to prayer and rewards for simple obedience.

The main way to avoid disappointment in marriage is to set our hope fully on the grace to be brought to us at the revelation of Jesus Christ.[190] He understands, and only he understands. He loves us unconditionally, and only he loves us that way. He will give us grace to serve him in this life, and will grant us unlimited bliss forever in a new heaven and a new earth. He will wipe away every tear from our eyes, and fill us with unending joy and gladness.[191] Marriage is one aspect of our pilgrimage, and an important one, but it's not the sum and substance of life. Christ alone is our life.[192] My hope and prayer is that you will avoid most common marital troubles and build a truly beautiful relationship, to the glory of God. Although there is no completely happy marriage in this life and in this world, there will be one in the next life, when we all sit down together for the marriage supper of the Lamb.[193]

Conclusion

As the Presbyterian *Book of Common Worship* says, God "established marriage for the welfare and happiness of humankind." The Anglican *Book of Common Prayer* states that marriage "is an honourable estate, instituted by God, signifying unto us the mystical union that is betwixt Christ and his Church: which holy estate Christ adorned and beautified with his presence and first miracle that he wrought in Cana of Galilee."

God designed marriage for our happiness, and those who follow his revealed will about this relationship will enjoy a substantial degree of physical, emotional, social, spiritual, and perhaps even financial well-being in this life.[194]

---

190 1 Pet 1:13.

191 Revelation 21:3.

192 Col 3:3.

193 Revelation 19:9.

194 This is a general principle. There are many exceptions, such as in time of war, natural disaster, financial collapse, and personal illness. Still, married people who trust God and seek to follow his ways will generally be happier even in this situations than others will be.

Even more important, God has given us marriage for the purpose of manifesting his own glory – his goodness, truth, and beauty. A man and woman who live together in lifelong faithfulness and who trust in God and endeavor to live according to his will as revealed in the Bible will both experience and reflect God's inherent goodness. They will reflect the loving relationship between the Father and the Son, and they will manifest the relationship between Jesus Christ and his church.

If, then, we make the glory of God our main goal for our marriage, we will taste and see the goodness of God, and others will be drawn to praise and honor God because of what they see in us. As Paul said, "Whatever you do, do all to the glory of God."[195]

What I have written represents a little of what I have learned from books, my own experience, and the experiences of couples with whom I have spoken over the years. Much more could be said, and has been, by people far more qualified than I am. I hope you will make it habit to read at least one book on marriage each year; you can start with the list at the end of this volume.

---

195 1 Cor 10:31.

APPENDIX 1

THE BIBLE AND DIVORCE

More and more marriages are terminating in divorce. In every case, one or both parties believe that divorce is preferable to staying together in an unhappy marriage. The pain of living together is so great that permanent separation seems to be the only choice. With the support of family, friends, the media, even church leaders, couples decide that it would be better to sever the marriage bond.

No one—and certainly not those who are married! — disagrees that marriage is difficult, and that building a relatively happy marriage takes years of hard work. Nor does anyone deny that marital conflict cuts to the heart and leaves painful inner wounds.

What most people don't know, however, is that a strong case can be made against divorce. I am not just talking about the teaching of the Bible, which is clear enough, despite the confusion reigning in the church on this issue nowadays. "For the LORD God of Israel says that he hates divorce... Therefore, take heed to your spirit, that you do not deal treacherously" (Malachi 2:16).

Marriage creates a one-flesh union between a man and a woman. Although they may separate, this union cannot really be broken. Psychological studies have shown that any separation of husband and wife—through divorce or death—generates profound confusion, grief, and sadness. This union occurs when a man and a woman publicly commit themselves to each other, live together, engage in sexual intercourse, and work together. The bond thus forged lasts for a lifetime. Thus, changing marriage partners is not like changing clothes, as some erroneously believe.

Because man and wife are one, they can bring each other either great joy or bitter sorrow. We are hurt most by those closest to us. No one is closer than our mate; that is why marital conflict produces such anguish.

Marriage, even when there is conflict, bestows many benefits: companionship, help, security, extended family, new friends, and division of labor at home, to name only a few. Sexual pleasure adds to the delight of living with someone. For men, sexual intercourse fulfills a powerful drive, one which can dominate a man's life. For women, it can bring pleasure, release from tension, and a sense of being loved and desired. Sexual frustration, on the other hand, causes profound tension, especially in the man, but also in the woman.

God intended marriage to result in children. To carry on the human race. He ordained that new life should begin in a home with a father and a mother. He further planned that children should grow up in a stable home with two parents, as recent studies have proven.

The Purpose of Pain

But what about the pain of marriage, to which we referred above? The benefits we can easily understand; they drew us to marriage to begin with. But the awful feelings accompanying conflict—or even just lack of intimacy—what are we to do with these? Do they not prove that we made a mistake and married the wrong person, or that the union should be terminated?

Here many people go wrong. They do not comprehend the role of pain in life, including married life. In a perfect world, pain would not exist. But in this fallen world, populated by sinners, pain plays a vital role. Walter Trobisch, the famed marriage counselor of a previous generation, used to say that "Growth is connected mostly with pain."

God intends for his people to grow up into maturity, into

the "measure of the stature of the fullness of Christ".[196] That is, our Father wants us to become like his Son Jesus. That means that we must learn how to love as Christ loved, laying down his life for his friends, giving himself, sacrificing himself.

We come into this world infected with sin, a chief trait of which is profound selfishness. When we love, we deny ourselves for the good of another. We are also naturally filled with unbelief in God's goodness and power. When we trust him, we receive both his love and his power to love others through us. As Martin Luther said, marriage is a "school for character." By living closely with someone whose personality, background, interests, desires, fears, and hopes differ so radically from ours, we must learn to love. But that means sacrificing ourselves. And that means pain.

If we run from the pain, we shall never learn to love and we shall never grow up. We shall remain infants, pre-occupied with ourselves, demanding instant gratification of our own wants, regardless of the cost to others. Have you ever noticed how her baby's cry immediately captures a mother's full attention? God meant it that way. In the same fashion, the pain of conflict with our marriage partner engages us. We can't ignore it. If we run towards pain, seeking the cause and, relying on God's help, dealing with the problem, we shall grow through pain to maturity. If we run away, we shall lose the opportunity to experience God's power and love.

But we shall never love perfectly, nor shall we ever be fully loved by another. Marriage confronts us with that sobering fact within a short time after the wedding. God knew that, too. He uses marriage (and other close relationships) to remind us that only he can fulfill our longing for unconditional love. When we feel the limited acceptance, or even rejection, of those close to us, God invites us into his own gracious presence, where we shall receive his boundless affection.

Likewise, when we confront the reality of our own pride, laziness, fear, selfishness, and even malice, we can turn to God for forgiveness. Jesus has died for sinners, so that we can be

---

196 Eph 4:13.

reconciled to God. Failure to love others can drive us to the cross, where God's love meets our hardness of heart and melts us, again and again.

Paradoxically, by confessing our faults and receiving God's mercy, we find new energy to extend mercy to others. In other words, our own failure—if turned over to God for his transforming work—can equip us to grant pardon and compassion to our spouse.

All these blessings we lose if we give up and march into the divorce court.

The Biblical Teaching on Divorce and Remarriage

When we are tempted to consider divorce, we need to reflect anew on what the Bible teaches. Particularly, we must understand God's plan for marriage (as described earlier in this book), so that we can understand his opposition to divorce.

Here are the main passages explicitly dealing with divorce and remarriage after divorce.

The words of Jesus:

"Whoever divorces his wife for any reason except fornication causes her to commit adultery; and whoever marries a woman who is divorced commits adultery."[197]

"Have you not read that he who made them at the beginning 'made them male and female,' and said, 'For this reason a man shall leave his father and mother and be joined to his wife, and the two shall become one flesh'? So then, they are no longer two but one flesh. Therefore, what God has joined together, let not man separate... Whoever divorces his wife, except for fornication, and marries another, commits adultery; and whoever marries her who is divorced commits adultery."[198]

"Whoever divorces his wife and marries another commits adultery against her. And if a woman divorces her husband and marries another, he commits adultery."[199]

"Whoever divorces his wife and marries another commits

---

197 Matt 5:32.
198 Matt 19:4-6, 9.
199 Mk 10:11-12.

adultery; and whoever marries her who is divorced from her husband commits adultery." [200]

The words of the Apostle Paul:

"The woman who has a husband is bound by the law to her husband as long as he lives. But if the husband dies, she is released from the law of her husband. So then, if, while her husband lives, she marries another man, she will be called an adulteress; but if her husband dies, she is free from that law, so that she is no adulteress, though she has married another man." [201]

"Now to the married I command, yet not I but the Lord: A wife is not to depart from her husband. But even if she does depart, let her remain unmarried or be reconciled to her husband. And a husband is not to divorce his wife. But to the rest I, not the Lord, say: If any brother has a wife who does not believe, and she is willing to live with him, let him not divorce her. And if a woman who has a husband who does not believe, if he is willing to live with her, let her not divorce him. ... But if the unbeliever departs, let him depart; a brother or sister is not under bondage in such cases. But God has called us to peace." [202]

"A wife is bound by law as long as her husband lives; but if her husband dies, she is at liberty to be married to whom she wishes, only in the Lord." [203]

It would seem that these passages are plain enough, but several different interpretations have arisen among Christians:

There are no grounds for divorce. Remarriage after divorce amounts to adultery.

There is one legitimate cause for divorce: Fornication, which is defined either as premarital sexual relations or marriage to a close relative; if either of these is discovered after marriage, divorce is lawful. Remarriage after such a divorce is not lawful in God's eyes.

There are two grounds for divorce: Adultery, and separation.

---

200 Lk 16:18.
201 Rom 7:2-3.
202 1 Cor 7:10-13, 15.
203 1 Cor 7:39.

Remarriage after such a divorce is allowed by God.

There is more to adultery than a physical relationship with someone other than your spouse, and more to separation than physically leaving. Thus, anything which shows a profound lack of commitment to the marriage constitutes either adultery or separation and offers suitable grounds for a biblical divorce.

Although Christians may not divorce (or remarry after divorce), Christians who were divorced before they believed in Christ are fully forgiven and free to re-marry.

As we consider this vital subject, we need to remember several facts:

When Matthew uses the word "fornication" [sometimes translated as "sexual immorality"] he does so differently from Paul. He carefully distinguishes adultery (unfaithfulness of someone who is married) from fornication (sexual sin before marriage). Thus, any interpretation which fails to take note of this distinction will miss the point of Jesus' teaching.

Jesus, while allowing divorce for "fornication," explicitly forbids remarriage after divorce, and he does so in the clearest possible language.

Paul states clearly that married people are bound to each other until death.

In 1 Corinthians 7, Paul, while allowing the believer not to contest the departure of an unbelieving mate, does not grant the right to re-marry, but at the end of the chapter explicitly says that married people are bound to each other until death.

Contemporary Jews allowed divorce and remarriage for all sorts of reasons. Jesus obviously meant to distinguish his teaching from theirs. His words could not have been much clearer. Moses gave a commandment about divorce and remarriage (Deuteronomy 24) to limit the sin that formerly married people could commit against each other, but Jesus clearly attributed this to man's hardness of heart. "Hardness of heart" in the Bible almost always describes a condition of those who do not believe in God, do not obey God, and are destined for eternal wrath.

Adultery, while devastating to a relationship, does not break the bond or kill the marriage. If that were the case, Israel's constant unfaithfulness to her God, often termed "adultery," would have severed the covenant with God, which it did not. The entire book of Hosea makes this one point. God never divorced Israel, though she was frequently unfaithful to him and never loved him as he loved her. He remained faithful to a wicked wife. Likewise, Jesus has bound himself forever to a church that constantly wanders away into sin. How could he allow Christians to do otherwise?

There is a difference between forgiveness of sins and responsibility for the consequences of our actions. We live in a moral universe; God does not repeal his moral laws for his children. Therefore, when we sin—and we all do—and confess our sins with faith in the death of Christ for our forgiveness, God fully pardons us. But we shall have to live with the consequences of our sins, as David did after he committed adultery with Bathsheba. One of the consequences of divorce for a believer is loss of freedom to marry again.

Jesus and Paul make no distinction at this point between believers and non-believers. In fact, Jesus makes it clear that God's order for marriage began at creation, and thus applies to all men and women. We cannot apply one principle to people before, and another after, they believe. What we do as non-believers has consequences for our life as believers. People who crippled their bodies by reckless driving before coming to faith in Christ will have to live with their disability, just as those who divorced as unbelievers will have to remain single. In each case, God will provide sufficient grace to serve him with joy.[204]

Moses in Deuteronomy 24 (a passage often cited in defense of the right to marry after divorce) says that a divorced woman who marries another has been "defiled." The most natural interpretation of this is that she has done what she should not have done by marrying another man after having been divorced.[205]

When Jesus says that not all can receive his teaching, he referred not to the binding nature of his laws about divorce and

---

204 2 Cor 12:9.
205 Deut 24:1-4.

remarriage, but to his saying that some people deliberately forego marriage so "for the kingdom of heaven's sake," as the punctuation in the New King James Version indicates.[206]

Thus, I accept the second position named above, although I respect the first one; all the others I consider to be improper interpretations of the Biblical passages. That is, There is one legitimate cause for divorce: Fornication, which is defined either as premarital sexual relations or marriage to a close relative; if either of these is discovered after marriage, divorce is lawful. Remarriage after such a divorce is not lawful in God's eyes.

But that is the teaching of the Bible, and most people don't accept the Bible as their authority for making decisions. Are there any other reasons why divorce is not wise or beneficial, why it is harmful for those who choose that way? Yes.

---

206 Matt 19:11-12.

APPENDIX 2

THE PSYCHOLOGICAL CASE AGAINST DIVORCE

Diane Medved, a secular psychologist, once set out to write a book defending divorce as the lesser of two evils for many married people. When she had completed her research, however, she published an entirely different work, *The Case Against Divorce*.[207] I briefly summarize some of her points below. Numbers in parentheses refer to pages in her book.

As she did her research, she discovered that "divorce was catastrophic – but not in the commonly accepted terms of a simple year or two thrown away... The physical act of packing a bag and moving out is traumatic. And from there on the trauma escalates." "People could be spared enormous suffering if they scotched their permissive acceptance of divorce and viewed marriage as a serious, lifelong commitment" (4).

She learned about "the permanent distrust, anguish, and bitterness divorce brings" (4) and discovered the "lingering emotional and psychological effects." "Women's standard of living declines by... 73 percent in the first year after divorce." Most women who get divorces are still clinically depressed ten years after the divorce, and all "were moderately or severely lonely." The chances of divorced women finding another husband are less than those of "being struck by a terrorist!" (6)

---

207 Diane Medved, *The Case Against Divorce* (New York: Donald I. Fine, Inc, 1989)

"The effects of divorce last a lifetime. And they are in actuality far worse than we care to confront" (7).

She herself is divorced and, though happily remarried, writes poignantly of the "enormous loss" of her divorce. Her second marriage is an exception, for only one-half of those she interviewed who remarried stayed with the second spouse or found themselves happy in their new marriage (actually, the percentage nationwide is much lower).

"No one ever emerges from a divorce unscathed—he or she is inevitably permanently harmed" (10). She reviews the usual reasons for divorce and agrees that "after divorce women especially, and men to some extent, report emotional growth. But they won't admit that they might have blossomed even more had they gathered the gumption to stick with and heal the marriage" (12).

In brief, her "case against divorce" includes four elements, which I quote in full:

Divorce hurts you. Divorce brings out selfishness, hostility, and vindictiveness. It ruins your idealism about marriage. It leaves emotional scars from which you can never be free. It costs a bunch of money—and significantly reduces your standard of living.

Divorce hurts those around you. It devastates your children for at least two years and probably for life. It hurts your family by splitting it in two; both family and friends are compelled to take sides. It forces you to be hardened against people you once loved. It rips the fabric of our society, each divorce providing another example of marriage devalued.

The single life isn't what it's cracked up to be. Ask anyone—the "swinging singles" life is full of frustration, rejection, and disappointment. The Mr. or Ms. Right you assume waits for you may be only a futile fantasy. Even a successful affair that bridges you from one marriage to another often becomes merely a second failure.

Staying married is better for you. You don't have to disrupt your life for two to seven years; instead, solving marital problems provides a sense of teamwork and stands as a concrete accomplishment that enhances problem-solving skills in the larger world. Marriage is statistically proven to be the best status for your health, divorce the worst. Marriage gives you something to show for your time on earth – children (usually) and a bond built on continuity and history (13).

Dr. Medved spends the rest of her book substantiating and illustrating her thesis with a multitude of statistics and personal stories. She surveys the usual reasons for seeking divorce and finds them insufficient grounds for inflicting such permanent damage on yourself and your family. She then gives seven reasons for staying together, including:

- The welfare of the children (recent studies have added more weight to her argument that divorce devastates children).[208]
- The power of perseverance.
- The value of keeping a long-term relationship together.
- The damage done to family and friends by divorce.
- The consequences of divorce are too awful.
- The desire not to hurt one's spouse.
- The fear of being alone.

Then she mentions the "costs of divorce." Here are some of the section headings:

---

208 See, for example, https://www.focusonthefamily.com/marriage/divorce-and-infidelity/should-i-get-a-divorce/how-could-divorce-affect-my-kids

- "The Emotional Impact of Divorce: Much Pain, No Gain"
- "A Very Special Private Hell"
- "Hurting the One You Love"
- "Becoming a Lesser Person"
- Being "Crazy in Our Midst"
- "The Alluring Vitality of Anger"
- "Divorce Won't Solve Your Problems"
- "Doomed to Repeat the Past"
- "A Blow to Self-Esteem"

In her last section, Medved surveys a few of "The Benefits of Staying Married":

- "Only Marriage Brings True Romance"
- "Marriage Is Good for Your Character"
- "Marriage Meets Our Need for Attachment"
- "Marriage is a Safe Haven"
- "Strength Comes Through Crisis"
- Marriage is "The Only True Commitment"
- Marriage is "The Ultimate Setting for Fulfilling Life's Purpose" (The above are all from the Table of Contents)

APPENDIX 3

WHAT SHOULD WE DO WITH A DIFFICULT MARRIAGE?

If divorce (and thus remarriage) is not an option for God's people, and there is so much evidence of the negative psychological effects of divorce, that leads to the obvious question: What, then, should we do with a difficult marriage?

First of all, we need to understand that *all* marriages are difficult! People often think that only they are having marital problems when, in fact, all married couples do. We are selfish sinners and will inevitably encounter conflict with each other.

Then, we need to ask, What is God trying to teach me? How does he want me to grow in faith, hope, and love? How does my spouse's sin show me my own sin? How does his or her criticism point up my fault? How would Jesus love this person? As we seek God's wisdom, we shall find that we need his help. We shall see our sin more clearly, and our need for his forgiveness and his power to love the unlovely.

That will drive us to prayer and to the Bible. In prayer, we should confess our own sins, asking God's forgiveness and his love for our mate. Then we should pray for our partner, asking God to forgive him or her and change him or her.

We should find some other person of the same sex with whom we can pray. But be careful! Don't spend time criticizing or complaining about your mate. Instead, ask your friend to pray for *you*. Confess your own faults and ask for prayer. Admit that your love and patience are running out, and beg them to call upon God to give you his strength. You will find that mutual prayer will give you strength to go on.

Of course, we need to go to church regularly. By worshiping God with others, we shall forget our own troubles for a while and concentrate upon the greatness and the goodness of God. In church, we remember why God made us—to know and glorify him, not to have a "happy" life on this earth. Get into a small group Bible study. Seek out a marriage counselor and keep going until you can communicate with each other without fighting.

Find some Bible passages that speak to your difficulty. Husbands, if your wife is contentious—and most wives *are* sometimes contentious—then meditate upon those Bible passages which speak of returning evil with good, being patient, gentle and kind, and the duty of the husband to love his wife as Jesus loved the church (like Ephesians 5:22-33). Wives, if your husband is unloving—and most husbands *are* sometimes unloving—then focus upon those passages of the Bible which remind us that Jesus is the only source of unconditional love, and those which require wives to submit to their husbands, even non-Christian ones (like 1 Pet 3:1-6).

It is good for us to submit to God's discipline. Through marriage, he disciplines us, to cause us to grow more loving and to trust him more. Remember, too, that marriage lasts only for a few years. When we die, we shall no longer be married, except for our union with Christ. Knowing that we have ahead of us an eternity of delight will encourage us to ask God to enable us to endure a few more years of difficulty in this life.

At the same time, we should try to be thankful. No one is totally evil all the time. Think of your spouse's good points, and meditate upon those, with thanksgiving to God. Speak works of encouragement and gratitude to your partner; this will encourage him or her to keep doing what you like. Nagging and criticism do no good, nor do they change the other person. After you have expressed your preferences once, take them to God in prayer and ask him to change your spouse. Your words of disapproval will only make the situation worse. Believe me—I speak from experience! Rather than concentrating upon the faults and failings of your spouse, ask God for strength to do your duty as a married person. Husbands, love your wives as Christ loved the church and gave himself for her; men must sacrifice for their wives. Wives, submit to your husbands as the church submits to Christ. Show him respect and serve him, and your life with him will be happier.

We could go on and on, but these few suggestions are enough to show how we should begin to deal with a difficult marriage—which is a normal one! As we turn to him, God will grant us all the grace we need to do his will, which is to stay together.

APPENDIX 4

Brief Replies to Some Common Reasons for Wanting a Divorce

At the risk of seeming cold and hard-hearted, I would like to give very brief responses to some of the reasons that people have expressed to me for initiating divorce. I do this as a sort of reality check, to challenge some assumptions and hopefully to encourage people to re-think their views of marriage.

"My marriage is dead. My spouse's behavior killed it." You often hear this statement in Evangelical circles, where it is usually combined with the idea that "the marriage bond has been broken" by adultery or desertion or some chronic behavior indicating low commitment to the marriage.

The major problem with this concept is that you can't find it in the Bible. The relationship surely suffers terrible damage by adultery, drug abuse, addiction to pornography, hateful words, and other signs of lack of love, but does it "die"? In the Bible, this metaphor is not used. God, as we have seen, remained faithful to his spouse, Israel, even when she had "broken" the "covenant." He would not give up until, like Hosea, he had won her back. The relationship may be damaged and filled with excruciating pain, but it is not "dead."

"There is no hope of reconciliation." How do you know? As long as you persist in seeking God's grace in your life, there is hope that he will change you enough to forgive your spouse, ask forgiveness from your spouse, and even for both of you to come to a new place of mutual respect and acceptance. Even if your spouse has remarried, you don't have to; your faithfulness to your original marriage vow can stand as a sign of God's faithfulness to us, his erring children.

"My spouse has no intention of preserving this marriage." That may be the case, but do you then have to make sure that it ends in divorce? Perhaps if you showed more humility and patience, your spouse would come around. Perhaps not; maybe your spouse is so hard-hearted that reconciliation will never take place. But you don't have to be the one who shuts the door.

"My marriage is a sham." What do you mean? That your marriage appears better than it is? Most marriages do. We don't—and shouldn't—share all our secrets with others. On the other hand, perhaps someone needs to know about your troubles in order to help you. Find a marriage counselor; get into a couples group where you can express some of your difficulties. Find one person of the same sex with whom you can admit your lack of love for your spouse and pray about it.

"God does not want me to live forever in an unhappy marriage." There are several possible responses to this assertion:

God *does* promise that certain people will be "happy" (usually translated as "blessed") in this life. Notice to whom those promises are given: Those who turn away from sin, follow God's law, and live out the Beatitudes (re-read Matthew 5:3–12 to refresh your memory if necessary). To the degree that we violate God's will, to that degree this "happiness" will not be ours. Divorce violates his will.

Jesus promised, "In this world you will have trouble."[209] Paul tells us in Romans 8:22 that this whole universe groans in pain, awaiting the return of Christ and the redemption of our bodies form sin. Until then, there is no undiluted "happiness" for anyone on this earth. Those who set their hopes on earthly happiness will suffer sharp disappointment.

True happiness comes from holiness. God wants us to be

---

209 John 16:33.

holy. He often uses "unhappiness"—illness, poverty, rejection, sorrow—to refine us and make us more like his Son Jesus. Our marital struggles—and all married people have them—are a part of his gracious work to reveal our sin and his forgiveness and demonstrate his transforming power. That will produce Christian joy, which is much deeper and more lasting than worldly "happiness."

"I can't stand the pain anymore." The agony of marital strife is truly awful, perhaps especially so for women. Sometimes, it all seems to be just too much. The Psalmist often called out to God to help him speedily, because it often seems that God has already "delayed" too long. On the other hand, both the Bible and history tell us that people can people can take far more pain than they realize. Paul suffered extreme agonies of body and soul, so that he felt he was close to death, but God delivered him.[210] Out of his experience, he learned that God's grace is sufficient for us each day, and that his power is made manifest in our weakness.[211] Perhaps God can use your pain to drive you closer to himself, so that you see your sin and his grace, and begin to experience his transforming power. Remember the words of Paul, "I can do all things in him who strengthens me" (spoken to a different situation, but applicable to all believers), and "God is faithful, [who] will not allow you to be tempted beyond what you are able, but with the temptation will also make the way of escape, that you may be able to endure it."[212]

"I can't take the uncertainty of not knowing whether we'll ever be reconciled; I would prefer the certainty of divorce." That is understandable, but remember that uncertainty is a sign of life. The certitude of divorce is the certitude of death. It is final, irreversible, and far worse than you imagine. We can only find security and certainty in the promises of God to be with us and to supply us with all the strength we need for each day. We know that he is working all things together for our good, and that

---

210 2 Cor 1:8-11.
211 2 Cor 12:9.
212 1 Cor 10:13.

nothing can separate us from his love for us in Christ.[213] We can't be sure whether we'll ever be reconciled with our spouse, but we can be sure that we are reconciled with God through Jesus Christ, and that he will give us all we need for each day. Psalm 23 provides us with words of certain hope that our Good Shepherd will take good care of us and, even in the valley of the shadow of death, be with us to protect us and provide for us.

"I made a mistake when I married this person. Now I want to correct that error and get on with life." You may have made an unwise, immature, uninformed, even foolish decision, but God makes no mistakes. Your decision was part of his plan for your life. He works "all things" together for your good, if you love him. Your past folly does not frustrate his design to conform you to Christ, mostly through suffering.[214]

"Why should I have to live forever with the consequences of a poor choice?" Because that is the way God has constituted this moral universe: Actions have consequences. On the other hand, if we will repent of our sins, including the sin of a hasty or foolish marriage choice, then we can experience God's renewing, redeeming, abundant mercy and power in our lives. He brings good out of evil—witness the Cross, for example. If we turn to him in constant faith, he will grant us such a relationship with himself that we shall know his love and power more and more each day. Who knows? Perhaps your spouse will see a change in you and want to have what you have.

"I've learned from my mistake. When I marry the next time, I'll do things better." You should rather say, "*If* I marry again—the odds are not as great as you imagine. Then, you should say, "I *hope* I'll do better," for if you failed one time, you will most likely fail again. Further: Have you really learned from your mistake? What have you learned? To persevere under trials, confessing your sin and asking God's love to fill your heart and overflow to those around you, or to cut and run when the going gets too tough?

---

213 See Rom 8:28, 31-39.
214 Rom 8:29-30.

The bottom line is that God seeks our holiness.[215] Given our fallen nature, he usually employs pain as his primary means of changing us.[216] We can either cooperate with his chastening of us and learn what he seeks to teach us or turn from his loving discipline and seek to go our own, pain-free, way. If we do refuse his chastening in our lives, we shall merely meet his loving resistance again and again, until we finally bow before him in humble faith and submission to his will.

God sends difficult people into our lives to uncover our hidden idols and then to deliver us from them through reliance on his grace in Christ. If we cooperate with him, we shall find increasing liberation from sin and freedom in his love. If we turn from him, we shall continue in bondage to gods that are not gods, especially the elusive idol of "happiness."

Please forgive me if my words sound cold and heartless. I am aware that longstanding, chronic emotional pain can wear one down, and that marital conflict is perhaps the most excruciating relational suffering there is. I don't want to minimize your heartache and agony.

On the other hand, I've seen God work miracles in many marriages, including my own (though we were never at the point of even considering divorce), and I know that he is able to reach down into the miry pit and pull us out.[217] He can also bear us up each day with his tender love and care. He will never leave us or forsake us.[218] As long as we look to him in faith, even desperate faith, he will not disappoint us. He may not heal your marriage, but he can heal your heart and give you joy amidst severe trials.[219] And someday, God himself will wipe away every tear from our eyes.[220] As we keep our eyes fixed on Jesus, he will refresh us with his own death-defeating energy and life, until he comes to take us home.[221]

---

215 Eph 1:4; Col 1:22; 1 Pet 1:16.
216 Heb 12:3-11.
217 See Ps 40:1-3.
218 Heb 13:5. See also Matt 28:20.
219 1 Pet 1:6-7.
220 Rev 7:17.
221 Heb 12:2.

APPENDIX 5

DEALING WITH PAST DIVORCE AND REMARRIAGE

We need to address the very real situation of those who have already been divorced. They know pain that the rest of us do not, and need special comfort from God. Here are a few brief guidelines:

All who repent of their past sins and believe in Christ receive full forgiveness. Divorce and remarriage—and all the sins which cause these actions—can be forgiven by God.

Those who harbor resentment do not enjoy God's favor. Divorced people need to forgive their former spouses. If they have not remarried, they need to seek reconciliation.

Although they can be admitted to communion, men who are divorced (or remarried after divorce) cannot serve as elders or deacons in the church.[222]

We should all deal gently with people who have gone through divorce or remarriage. They are our fellow sinners; we are no better than they are; if we are self-righteous, we are even worse than they are! We should look to ourselves, asking God to keep us from all sorts of sins, including sins against marriage, for this is an institution much beloved by God.

---

222 1 Tim 3:2, 12; Tit 1:6.

APPENDIX 6

OVERCOMING INFIDELITY

I'll never forget the first time I encountered adultery. It was 1974, and I was still in graduate school after having served as pastor of three small churches for a couple of years. Friends from our new church had called us in the middle of the night, asking us to come to their home quickly. When we entered the apartment, we saw the young wife, clad in her nightgown, sitting on the couch with her head down. Her husband stood over her with an expression of agony on his face. He had discovered that she had had an affair with a friend of theirs.

Since then, I have listened to many stories of marital infidelity of various types. A mature husband and father confessed to having succumbed to the wiles of a prostitute in a hotel overseas. A young man told how, after suffering terrible treatment from his new wife for two years, he had found a woman who truly loved him. They had already slept together, and he was contemplating leaving his wife for this person. A Christian leader told of how he had "come close" to intercourse with different women over the years, though he had never committed the act of marriage with them. Several husbands were addicted to Internet pornography. A wife suddenly discovered messages on her husband's iPhone revealing that he had been engaging in same-sex activity for several years.

Regardless of the form that infidelity takes, the effect on one's spouse is nothing less than devastating. The whole world comes crashing down. Trust is utterly shattered. You feel betrayed, abandoned, treated like dirt. An awful future looms up before you. What will become of the marriage now? The children? How can you ever return to a "normal" life after such an outrageous offense?

Reaction

The process of recovery will take time and cannot be rushed. The offended spouse will respond with outrage, grief, hurt, disbelief, sorrow, self-doubt, and a variety of emotions that must be expressed. We must give time and "space" for the venting of these feelings, without minimizing, judging, correcting, or even reinforcing them unnecessarily.

Even when the guilty party apologizes, appears remorseful or repentant, and asks forgiveness, we should remind him or her that an immediate response may not be forthcoming from the spouse. It takes time for someone to begin to "settle down" emotionally enough even to hear such words, sincere though they may be. The adulterer must not imagine that things can return to normal quickly. He or she must rebuild trust over a period of months or even years, during which the enormity of the crime will, hopefully, become clearer, and the repentance deeper.

Repentance and reconciliation

Most spouses consider divorce as the only option, but I believe that we should ask God for divine help to move beyond the outrage, shock, and grief that infidelity causes and seek to re-build the relationship. That may seem impossible, but countless couples have been able to overcome the terrible damage of an affair – or any other form of infidelity – and avoid the heartache and lifelong wreckage that almost always follow divorce.

First, the person who has been unfaithful must admit his or her wrong, confess it as sin, and ask forgiveness from God and from his or her spouse. There are no excuses for adultery in any form. The sin must be dealt with by sincere repentance, sorrow, and an earnest request for mercy and transforming grace.

At the same time, he or she must take drastic steps to prevent a re-occurrence. Put blocks on Internet access to make watching pornographic material difficult. Get rid of all pornographic materials – DVDs, magazines, pictures, etc. – from the home and office. Cut off all communication with the person(s) involved in the adultery, whether they be a sexual partner (or more) or "friends" with whom the person has indulged in any form of lustful or tempting activity.

Stop going to any place associated with your sexual sin, including venues that arouse lust – movie theater; beach; swimming pool; gym; bar; rock concert – whatever reminds you of the sin or incites sinful desires.

Bring church leaders into this process as soon as possible. Call the pastor of your church; invite an elder or deacon to come to your home; tell the leader of your small group. You don't have to spread the news throughout the congregation, but a few key people need to step in and help the couple. Both the man and the wife will need the support of one or two godly people to meet with them at least weekly and pray with them. Find a marriage counselor to guide you through the initial stages of recovery and then to lead you into new habits of relating to each other.

I say, "relating to each other," because marital infidelity stems not just from the sinful heart and mind of the adulterer, but both impacts and reflects the whole marriage.

Here we need to be very careful. On the one hand, as I said, there is never any excuse for adultery. It is simply wrong, and responsibility for that sin rests squarely on the shoulders of the one who has been unfaithful.

On the other hand, most people who indulge in pornography or who form intimate relationships with someone other than their spouse do so out of a perception that something is lacking in their marriage. That is *not* to blame the other person for the sinful act. It is only to recognize that people who are more or less happy with their marriage, including the sexual aspect of it, are less likely to commit adultery than those who are highly dissatisfied. That is not always the case, but we should start with the assumption that the adulterer is looking for something "better" outside of marriage to make up for discontent with the relationship.

We all sense this intuitively, of course, but it underlies

the sub-title of Harley's book, *His Needs, Her Needs: How to Divorce-Proof Your Marriage.* Now, I don't think any marriage can be "divorce proof," for reasons that I'll explain later, but I do see where Harley gets this idea. He knows from experience that happily married people are much less "prone to wander" than are those who are neglecting to meet the legitimate desires of their spouse. You have probably talked with someone who failed to "walk the line" because their marriage was just too unsatisfying – or so they thought. They were sure that someone else would love them more, understand them better, and make them happier than their current (or former) spouse.

For this reason, we must ask ourselves, What could I have done better, to make it less likely for my spouse to want to go elsewhere for love and for sex? Without excusing another's sin, I should come before God with a humble heart, seeking to know how I have failed to reflect his love in my marriage and how I have made it harder for my spouse to keep his or her marriage vows.

Those who are trying to comfort and guide people reeling from the shock of their spouse's adultery should pray for wisdom here. At some point, they need to turn the eyes of the wounded person away from his or her pain and the sin of the spouse to their own failings as husband or wife. Friends and counselors should remind us that if we genuinely desire to love and serve God, he will show us where we have not glorified him in our marriage. He intends for us to grow in our knowledge of his grace and truth, and can use anything, even our spouse's adultery, to draw us closer to himself and deeper into the riches of his love for us in Christ.

Forgiveness

Sooner or later – and the sooner the better – the offended party must forgive the offender. This won't be easy, but God requires it of us, and has set us the supreme example by forgiving our sins.[223]

I have found that forgiveness comes much quicker when I have humbly asked God to show my own sins against him, and

---

223 See Eph 4:32-5:1

the ways in which I have committed spiritual adultery by seeking happiness in anyone or anything else but him. Perhaps I have made my marriage into an idol, investing more in it than I have in my relationship with God in Christ. I may have harbored critical or discounted thoughts about my spouse in my own heart, or may even have entertained fantasies of life with someone else. All too often, we fail to spend enough time together, or to build each other up with encouraging words and physical affection. None of us is a perfect marriage partner!

In any case, we have all "sinned and fall short of the glory of God."[224] "There is none righteous; no, not one."[225]

Rebuilding

Now is a good time to establish healthy patterns of communication, something that may have been lacking earlier. Set aside definite hours for reading books and articles about marriage together, perhaps this book on marriage; other occasions for honestly sharing matters that are causing conflict, in an atmosphere of mutual respect and listening; and still others for letting the Bible and other Christian literature – or films, podcasts, DVDs, or music – to refresh your spirits and your relationship.

Plan special occasions for relaxation and recreation, preferably wholesome physical activity outdoors, and get-togethers with Christian friends. You don't have to dwell on your marital problems at these times. Enjoying yourselves together will be enough and will replenish your emotional resources for the long journey ahead of you. Worship with other believers, and limited engagement in service, will re-orient your relationship around God and others. I say "limited" because we can become so busy helping others that you may neglect to nurture your marriage, which must be your first priority.

Marriage Counseling

In almost all cases, marriage counseling will be necessary.
Adultery in any form, including the use of pornography, both

224 Rom 3:23
225 Rom 9:10

reflects and causes serious fissures in the marriage relationship. Usually, couples cannot bridge these gaps by themselves. At the very least, they need a third party to moderate a series of conversations in which each person can express deeply held, and perhaps longstanding, opinions and complaints. Whereas we often can't do this without interruptions, disagreements, and emotional language and tone of voice that make further discussion impossible, sometimes the mere presence of another person forces us to maintain a relatively calm and courteous attitude.

The suggestions I've offered above only touch the surface of what couples reeling from the shock of adultery must address. Many hours of honest and respectful dialogue will be necessary to defuse the anger and remove the relational roadblocks that stand in the way of full reconciliation and the restoration – or, perhaps more accurately – the building, of a healthy marriage. I believe that skilled and trained counselors can play a vital role in this process, and strongly recommend that hurting couples do all they can to engage the assistance of such a person.

Because Christian and secular counselors operate from such widely divergent, even contradictory, assumptions, we should try to find someone who believes the Bible to be God's Word to shepherd us through the painful path to a better relationship. Even a non-Christian with training in marriage counseling can provide valuable assistance, however, as long as we hold to the biblical principles contained in the first part of this book.

Recognizing Strongholds

We must recognize, however, that only a deep work of God can get to the root of unfaithful thoughts and actions.

In such situations, the steps I mentioned above will not be enough. The deeper problem demands urgent attention.

APPENDIX 7

BREAKING FREE FROM SEXUAL "ADDICTIONS"[226]

Though a relatively happy marriage will reduce the temptations to adultery, the human heart is "deceitful above all things, and desperately wicked [or, *incurably sick*]; who can know it?"[227] We are all children of parents who were both finite and fallen. Others have also wielded influence upon us, especially in childhood and adolescence. Usually unwittingly, our parents and others did not love us as they should have. To be honest, we must admit that they did things, or failed to do things, that inflicted deep emotional wounds upon us and left us longing for love. Being inherently sinful, we all go "looking for love in all the wrong places," as the song says. Some of us, perhaps driven by an insatiable "love hunger," wander into dark alleys and encounter dangerous people.

We abet this destructive process by indulging our selfish desires and weaving a web of ungodly habits that grow stronger each time we entertain an unhealthy thought or engage in an act that violates God's revealed will. Eventually, we are slaves to something that seems to compel us towards what people now call addictions – that is, patterns of disordered desires and destructive

---

226 I put "addict" and "addiction" in quotation marks because, though we must face our utter inability to change ourselves, we must also believe that God has the power to break the chains that bind us and free us from slavery to even the worst obsessions, fears, and sinful patterns.

227 Jer 17:9

acts that we cannot break by our own power.

Our desperate search for love, security, excitement, meaning, and comfort in life often turns us away from God and toward someone or something else fill the aching void in our heart, quiet our fears, or otherwise dull the pain we all feel.

What we now call "addictions" come in many forms. We can give ourselves to food, entertainment, pleasure, alcohol, drugs, work, social media, adventure, an obsession with making money, politics – anything but God himself.

Addiction to pornography and illicit sexual activity often – indeed, in today's Internet world, increasingly - stem from these deep-seated systems of selfish gratification that the old theologians called "besetting sins." Adultery is a symptom of a much more serious condition: idolatry and the resulting slavery to our "idol."

Marital infidelity can destroy a marriage, or it can expose an underlying cancer and lead to treatment that brings greater emotional and spiritual health and produces a better marriage than before.

That is one reason why the relatively innocent party should demonstrate grace and patience, even while insisting upon genuine repentance and thoroughgoing reformation of lifestyle.

With the help of godly people, much prayer, and months and years of hard work, the "addict" can gain a new freedom to love, to live for others, and to deny self in order to find real and lasting happiness.

Still, we cannot underestimate the tenacity of addictions that stem from idolatry in the heart. They have put down roots that go deep and wide into our mind, body, and soul. They have us wounded, weak, and vulnerable. They tend to come in groups, so that the discovery of one addiction often leads to the recognition that you have another, or more. Each one demands our utmost attention and unremitting effort over a considerable time.

Here again, I strongly recommend that we call in outside help. People trained in guiding people towards recovery from various addictions can lead us, step by step, into greater and greater freedom. We must be willing to spend the time, effort, and money to obtain professional help.

Lest the relatively innocent party think that he or she has not idols or addictions, however, I remind you of what Jesus taught in Matthew 7:1-5. I may not be enslaved by food, drink, drugs, pornography, or sex, but do I look to people and things other than God for love, security, meaning, and other things that I crave? Almost surely, I do. Anything or anyone that I think I can't do without is an idol. Anyone or anything that occupies, or pre-occupies, my thoughts, my dreams, my fears, and my hopes is, effectively, a rival to God himself.

Writing to the Christians – Christians – in Corinth, Paul recalls the miserable conduct of the Israelites in the wilderness and warns, "And do not become idolaters as were some of them."[228]

Without minimizing the seriousness of obvious addictions, which can dominate and disrupt life and make normal relationships almost impossible, we must admit that we all have the potential to become slaves to some dominating sin. Let us treat each other with gentleness and humility, lest we also be tempted.[229] To quote the apostle Paul again, "Therefore let him who thinks he stands take heed lest he fall."[230]

Good books and online resources can supplement counseling. For those struggling with bondage to pornography and sex, I recommend *At the Altar of Sexual Idolatry*, by Steve Gallagher ;*Breaking Free,* by Russell Willingham; and *Surfing for God*, by Michael John Cusick.

As in the previous appendices, I emphasize that I have only given a very brief introduction to an enormously complex matter. I urge couples confronted with this monster to follow up with reading and help from skilled counselors, in faith that God can use the discovery of this kind of bondage to bring a new and even thrilling liberation for people formerly trapped by the world, the flesh, and the wiles of the devil. You can know fullness of life in Christ and you can enjoy the delights of marital sex, by the power of God!

---

228 1 Cor 10:7.
229 Gal 6:11-5.
230 1 Cor 10:12.

ABOUT THE AUTHOR

G. Wright Doyle received a B.A. in Latin from the University of North Carolina at Chapel Hill in 1966; a B.D. (M. Div.) from the Virginia Theological Seminary in 1969; and a PhD. in Classics from the University of North Carolina in 1975, with a dissertation on St. Augustine. He studied Mandarin Chinese at the Taipei Language Institute in Taiwan (1976–1978, 1980–1981). From 1980 to 1988, he taught Greek and New Testament at China Evangelical Seminary, Taipei.

From 1989 to 2015, the Doyles lived in Charlottesville, Virginia, where they reached out to Chinese Christians. In 2015, They moved to Texas. Wright now focuses on writing, encouraging and coaching people in the U.S., England, Taiwan, and China through telephone, Skype, and email. He continues to travel to Asia almost annually.

Wright is the author of *Reaching Chinese Worldwide* and *Christ the King*. He is the co-author of *China: Ancient Culture, Modern Society*; English editor of the *Biographical Dictionary of Chinese Christianity* (bdcconline.net); editor of *Builders of the Chinese Church*, editor and co-translator of *Wise Man from the East: Lit-sen Chang*; co-editor (with Dr. Carol Lee Hamrin) of the Wipf & Stock series, *Studies in Chinese Christianity*; and principal contributor to globalchinacenter.org and reachingchineseworldwide.org. He supervised the translation of Gingrich and Danker's Greek-English

Lexicon into Chinese, and prepared an abridgment of the Chinese edition of Carl Henry's *God, Revelation, and Authority.*

Wright has also written *Christianity in America: Triumph and Tragedy*; *Jesus:The Complete Man*; and *The Lord's Healing Words*. Seven of his books have been translated and published in Chinese.

RESOURCES

Some Helpful Books

It is important to note that no one should be obligated to agree with everything in any book, except the Bible. By listing these works, I do not endorse all that you will read in them. I am only saying that I have found these volumes to be useful in my understanding of marriage. I trust the reader to compare everything with the Scriptures, our only final authority.

My top picks

Christenson, Larry, *The Christian Family*. An older book, but full of wisdom.

Eggerichs, Emerson, *Love & Respect: The Love She Most Desires; The Respect He Desperately Needs*. A powerful call for following the biblical mandate to love and respect. It could revolutionize your marriage.

Harley, Willard F., Jr., *His Needs, Her Needs: Building an Affair-Proof Marriage*. A very helpful discussion of ways in which men and women's deepest desires differ, and how we can serve each other. Aside from the misleading title (we don't really "need" anything but God's love, and no marriage is affair proof), this book is extremely helpful. Some will object to his use of secular psychology, but I find that, as long as we rely on the Bible as our main authority, we can mine the results of psychological research for specific information that we can apply to marriage.

Keller, Timothy, with Kathy Keller, *The Meaning of Marriage*. An excellent all-around treatment of almost all aspects of marriage.

Mason, Mike, *The Mystery of Marriage*. A beautiful meditation on the profound mystery of marriage.

Stanley, Scott, Daniel Trathen, Savanna McCain, and Milt Bryan, *A Lasting Promise*. Biblical and practical advice on how to avoid destructive conflict and build a lasting marriage.

Marriage

Tournier, Paul, *To Understand Each Other*. Though very brief, this little book is profound and powerful. I recommend that all couples read it aloud to each other at least once a year.

Dealing with addictions to pornography and sex

Gallagher, Steve, *At the Altar of Sexual Idolatry*.

Willingham, Russell, *Breaking Free: Understanding Sexual Addiction & the Healing Power fo Jesus*.

Cusick, Michael John, *Surfing for God: Discovering the Divine Desire Beneath Sexual Struggle*.

Other good books

Adams, Jay, *Christian Living in the Home*.

Andrews, Robert. *The Family: God's Weapon for Victory*. Revised and updated Second Edition.

Bovet, Theodore, *Handbook to Marriage*.

Burkett, Larry, *Women Leaving the Workplace*.

Chapman, Gary, *The Five Love Languages: How to Express Heartfelt Commitment to Your Mate*.

Clark, Stephen, *Man and Woman in Christ*.

Crabb, Larry, *The Marriage Builder*.

Gray, John, *Men Are from Mars, Women Are from Venus*.

Medved, Diane, *The Case against Divorce.*

Piper, John, & Grudem, Wayne, *Recovering Biblical Manhood & Womanhood*

Sandford, John & Paula, *The Transformation of the Inner Man.*

CPSIA information can be obtained
at www.ICGtesting.com
Printed in the USA
FSHW011550140119
54858FS

9 781611 532937